The Membership Mindset

Challenges to change

SHANE McKEOGH

SAOR
Publishing

SAOR
Publishing

Saor publishing AUS/IRL
First published in Australia by Saor Publishing in 2016.
www.membershipmindset.com.au

Published by Saor Publishing under
the company name McKeogh Consultancy.

ISBN 0-646-96403-8 / 978-0-646-96403-4 (pbk)
ISBN 0-646-96440-2 / 978-0-646-96440-9 (ebook)

Dedication

This book is dedicated to all of those who have inspired me from day one – you know who you are!

For everyone who tells you that you can't, there will be someone who will tell you that you can. Listen to that someone.

Table of Contents

What is it all about?

About the author

Shane McKeogh is a fitness industry professional who has come up through a large organisation. He has worked his way up the corporate ladder with Goodlife Health clubs from sales all the way through to business management including everything in between. He was responsible for the corporate business connections in Western Australia, as the corporate sales and relationships manager and has come right the way through to the business manager of the entire region of Western Australia.

Shane grew up in Ireland during a recession and working in sales during this time was invaluable training for him on the values of a good work ethic as well as teaching him that hard graft gets results. His Irish heritage and the gift of the gab have been key factors that formed his ability to speak to almost anyone and, more importantly, to get on with anyone.

He will soon be marrying into fitness literally, as his partner Joanna is a fitness business owner who operates a successful business called 'The Fitness Pursuit'.

At the moment, Shane's life revolves firmly around the fitness industry, with a sneaky love for CrossFit. He was also involved in amateur boxing back in Ireland and has made many appearances in the ring again, working on the grit and graft within these two sports.

What does the author have to say for himself by way of a personal work life mantra? It's a very simple phrase. Work like a maniac.

Why are we here?

We all get into this industry for the right reasons (or at least we should), which is a firmly ingrained desire to help people. That is great, but there is so much more to it than that. This book will delve deeply into the inner workings of what it takes to work in the fitness industry from various points of view: the owner operator of a gym, a sales consultant, a personal trainer and everything in between. If you are involved in the realms of fitness, in any capacity, this is the book for you.

The book is laid out in short chapters, the points of which are summarised in a quick challenge at the end of each chapter. There are 42 challenges in total that will test and push you to be more than you are today. The idea is that you complete all of these challenges as you read, or directly after you have read the book in full; whichever way suits. In doing these challenges you will be able to guarantee that your skillset and knowledge (and hopefully your bank balance as well) will increase. This stems from my own personal mantra: do more, be more, see more.

The Membership Mindset will show you how to move away from a transactional thought process where you look at just one transaction at a time towards a process where you work on the longevity and lifecycle of a client. Our clients are our friends and we cherish friendships here.

This is not an instructional manual which tells you how to do a seated leg curl; it is a guide that will teach you how to survive and thrive in a hyper competitive industry. It will show you how to establish yourself as a dominating force and how to be a sales-savvy pro with rapport building skills that would rival the best politicians out there.

We are the fitness industry operators; we live in what I call the 'fitmosphere' – an atmosphere which revolves around fitness. We mould our lives around the simple practice of becoming healthier and fitter versions of ourselves; to me this is what living should be about. Get ready to be challenged every step of the way and to learn as you go. This book is not a test, but some of it may test you.

Do more, be more, see more.

Acknowledgments and thanks

My heartfelt thanks goes out to all of those who have helped me along the winding path, from support in my writing journey to business support and beyond.

Thank you to everyone who I have ever worked with, the good, the bad and the ugly – I have taken something from all of these individual experiences and many of your stories make up this book.

To you the reader, I say thank you for making this purchase and I truly hope you can use this book to learn how to excel in your business.

Of course my friends and family have supported me since day one, and I am eternally grateful to them. My parents have instilled in me what it is to work hard; thank you.

My little (not so little) brother who is a successful pilot at the age of 21. As you can tell, my parents instilled that work ethic in all of us!

Lastly my fitness pursuer Joanna Wilcox, my fiancée, my world and my raison d'être; without you none of this would be possible.

This book belongs to all of you as you are all the biggest part of it.

Goal Setting

'Guns shoot bullets,
bullets hit targets,
be a gun.'

Setting goals

I am going to start at the very beginning, with the setting of goals. Without goals you won't know where you're going and when you do know, you won't have a plan for how to get there. You wouldn't drive to a destination that you'd never been to before without entering the details into the satellite navigation first; the same goes for life. Enter your goals into the sat-nav of life.

Goal setting is crucial to ensure you are on the path to success. The fitness industry is an extremely tough business to make it in, with a PT churn rate of a year, at the best. Most of the people in your fitness education class won't even make it into the industry. Sales people often throw in the towel after just three months, mainly because they can't sustain their lifestyle on commission work and many management staff stress out after a short period of time, and leave.

Do these statistics sound familiar? Believe me; I see it in the industry every day. However, you do not have to be one of these statistics. Not if you stick it out. If you can last for more than six months, it will be half the battle and you'll be on your way to success.

I started my fitness career in membership sales and I quickly discovered that there was always one membership consultant on a revolving seat who couldn't hack it. I realised that if I just stayed the course I would get that consultant's leads once they left. It was easy to spot the ones who wouldn't last; they were wayward, had no self-direction and did not set goals. They had missed the point that all the management guidance or training in the world won't help if you don't actually show some true effort. Most of these people had sold themselves on the dream that is fitness but then the reality hit home hard and they couldn't cope with it.

Goal setting is about visualising where you will be and by when. Ensure your goals are tangible and that they can be tracked and monitored. I use a very simple goal setting system that has a big focus and a small focus. I draw these in circles to represent segments of my life and then I place that drawing someplace in my office in a highly visible position (See the drawing in the Challenge section). That way I can look at a micro goal (one-three months) and a macro goal (one year). I also make sure that the micro goals are all steps towards the macro goal(s).

Generally, I segment my life into six areas: job, finance, spiritual, health, key relationships (friends/family/fiancé-soon to be wife), and business. You decide what your 'sections' are and go from there, ensuring the micro goal falls within a one to three month timeframe where you can focus on and quantify your progress. The macro goal should have a timeframe of a year or more but you should also be able to quantify it, even though it's bigger, e.g. in the Health section my micro goal in 2015 was *make wiser food choices at tough times*' and my macro goal was to drop down to sub 10% body fat. The more conscious I was about my daily diet and nutrition, the easier it was to do cardio work as I felt lighter and not bloated. This in turn made it easier to drop fat and gain muscle as I could train for longer and more frequently.

Let me come back to my personal goal setting "drawings" with the circles for my life segments. The very first year I completed one of these life-saving, goal-setting documents was while I was sitting in an airport lobby. I had just read a great book, "*The One Thing*" by Gary Keller on the simple truth behind extraordinary results. By chance the only piece of paper I could find to write on was a bright yellow page, so I just used that to jot down my plan. Every year since then, I have deliberately made sure I use the same coloured paper to create this important document.

I'm a creature of habit but it also has the advantage that the colour helps this item stand out from every other piece of paper on show in my office. Feel free to use yellow paper or your own favourite coloured paper - as long as it works for you. Use it to mark this document out as an important document in your life. It could even be saved in an important documents folder on your desktop. What I am emphasising is that you will probably need to reference this strategic sheet any number of times, so make sure it is easily recognisable!

I use each of my six headings as visualisation pieces for each area of my life and I hold myself accountable to them daily. They remind me that without set goals you are simply meandering through life; you won't be able to establish the point where you have achieved what you wanted to.

Think of life in the fitness industry: you will have prede-termined key performance indicators (KPIs). PTs may have a goal for the number of sessions they need to run per week to pay the rent, salespeople may have a monthly sales target and management staff may have to focus on dollar value yield per membership. If you didn't decide what these goals were before attempting to achieve them, imagine how difficult it would be to know if you had succeeded or not. This is how you should be viewing yourself from here on out, as a business person operating in a business environment.

I can't emphasise enough the importance of goal setting as a way to improve both your business and yourself. If you have no goals, you cannot score. I am internally driven by my own tangible goals, which I have created myself. However, you will find some people need a friendly reminder of their goals from time to time and occasionally they may even want you to create their goals for them. Autonomy is vital in the world of goal setting, as you should want to establish your own personal goals. Nobody else really can understand how important a particular goal is to you; only you.

Challenge

So, you should have an idea of what is required to be a successful goal-setter now, and I have also described how you can look at your life closely and segment it as suits you. Now, I am going to set you a challenge, below.

Use the empty chart and fill it in with *your* six segments. You pick. You can use my examples; you can design your own; whatever is going to work for you. Be sure to set a micro focus (one-three months) and a macro focus (one-two years). The micro focus should always be a stepping stone to ensure you hit your macro focus points. Start with the most important section and move clockwise around the chart from the most important to least important. You might find that your goals have an equal importance - that's fine too, this isn't set in stone. Whatever works for you, do that!

Remember goal setting is personal and no one, besides you, can set your goals. Don't be scared to go BIG or to pick smaller goals that can be steady steps towards success. You decide.

MICRO/MACRO FOCUS GOALS graph

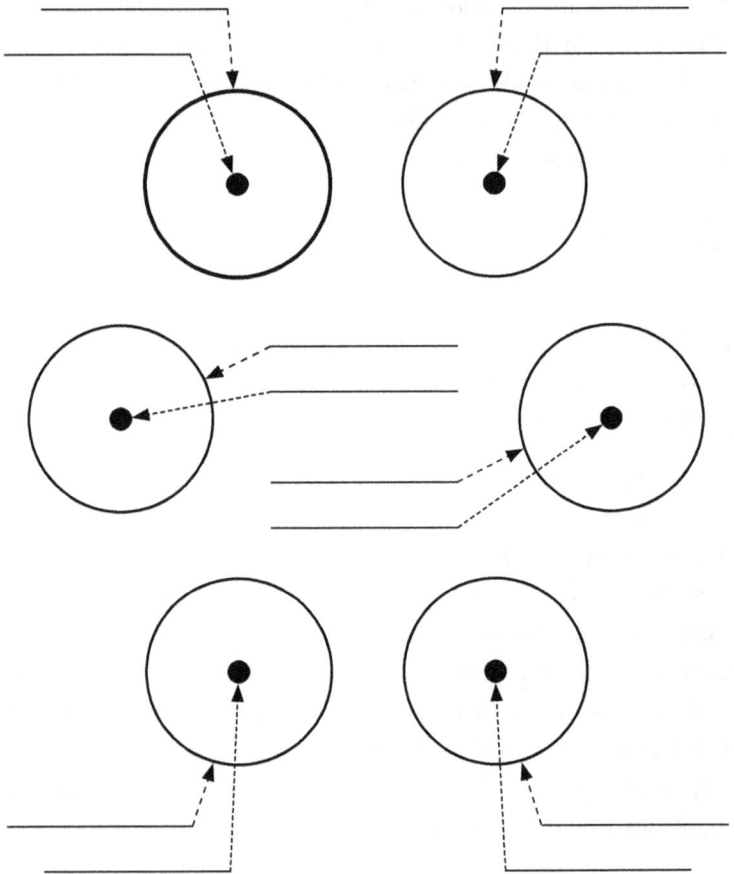

Yearly and daily

Goal setting is the starting point to ensuring that you set yourself up to achieve and to win. The next item on the agenda of choice is frequency. When you look at it like this it becomes very easy to see why some succeed and some just wander through their day.

Q. Which statement or sentence below describes you the most accurately?

a. Goal setting? What's that?

b. I goal set on a yearly basis or when I am forced to at work

c. I goal set on a quarterly basis

d. I goal set on a daily basis

For those who chose A, you need to have a serious conversation with yourself. For the rest of you just setting a goal at all is a good start - well done. The first step is underway; now you simply need to look at increasing that number to make it work for you.

For some people it is enough to set their goals once a year; as for me, I found that I forgot about what was important as more time passed. I needed to revisit my yellow document more often. Then I had that "click" moment where I realised that, in actual fact, I could just increase the number of times I set my goals. They were still the same goals but as a more visual person I discovered that if I wrote my goals down daily then that might make them more predominant in my day. Guess what? It worked. Now, instead of goal setting once a year, I rehash my goals twice a day (once in the morning and once in the evening). In essence I revisit my goals 730 times a year! Who do you think is more conscious of their daily goals?

I chose to make my daily focus about what I consider to be my most important 'life segment'. This in turn pushes it to the forefront of my life even more. In the morning, I write down my micro focus and in the evening I write down my macro focus, both concerning my most important life segment.

Things can change in an instant. I had some personal news, not long ago, which took me aback and which made me think how precious life really is and just how quickly things can change. That news made me realise that I need to know what I want to do, every day, because I do not know what the next day holds. Goal setting is great to do on a yearly basis however life is lived on a daily basis, so it needs to be viewed through the eyes of the goal setter, every day. You can let life get you down or you can let life lift you up; sometimes you are thrown a very difficult ball to catch and you must ensure you are ready to catch it, no matter the ferocity at which it is thrown. Prepare your goals like you prepare your dinner, every day and, hopefully, with some good ingredients.

Challenge

Can you try to increase your goal setting in ever-increasing increments: from yearly to quarterly to weekly to daily to twice per day? This can be done in one fell swoop or over time and just see if you don't become more conscious of your most important goal! You can note it in any medium: in your diary (see the next chapter), in your email calendar or on your phone - whatever way you see fit. You will be surprised what focusing on something over 700 times a year can do; you become so linked to your goal you can almost taste it. It is the first thing you think about when you get up in the morning and the last thing you visualise before you turn off for the day.

A Diary – get one

Do you have a little black book? Any of you who are in management should know how important this can be; from scheduling backups to documenting people issues and beyond. Your diary is your own work bible that you have created with passwords, conference call lines and other important information. You should have it with you, on hand, at all times. It can also be a friendly reminder tool; if your laptop or phone goes dead (yes, it happens!). At those moments, it becomes a solid back-up tool so no major appointment is ever missed.

Another great tool to use as a scheduler is your iPhone calendar. Ensure you use different coloured tabs for different sections; it might be red for clients, blue for personal, green for work etc. You decide and create the kaleidoscope that works for you.

Whilst these two tools are great for monitoring and for keeping you on track, they can also serve as a great way to make sure you can track backwards and review data and important issues. I always document my work travel in a log book, daily, and note any major purchases in my black journal. Don't forget, you can get a financial year diary as well as a calendar year diary.

Coming back to what we discussed earlier about visualising your goal setting, to me this is writing down my goal(s) in the morning at the top of my diary and at the bottom in the afternoon/evening. There are lots of cool modern ways to help you remember: you could email yourself, text yourself or use any other type of visualisation aid to help record your important goals.

You might find that you need to visualise a daily mantra or quote and so you could write this daily mantra at the top of your diary in the today section. Then when you are faced with a challenge you can remind yourself of your *raison d'être* for today!

Checklists and appointments can be 'ticked' off as you go – this is a great way to see what you are actually completing in comparison to what you set out to do. You PTs out there; look back at your day. How many reschedules did you have to make, what about cancellations, no shows, late clients etc. Could you use this information to help you predict future trends and to be one step ahead of the game? You see now, that if you don't look back, you can't move forward.

Just make sure you are not like me; countless times during my week, I accidently forget where I have left my diary. It is beyond me, the number of times I have nearly had a panic attack because I have left my journal lying around somewhere it shouldn't be. Now I have made a dedicated place where it must sit, so I have peace of mind. It is confidential after all.

Challenge

Go out today and buy a diary. It doesn't matter what date it is when you are reading this; it is never too late to plan. You don't need to be coming up to the New Year to plan.

OK, so you've purchased that new diary; now get to using it. Try to make sure you have an entry on the page for every day and make certain that it becomes an aide to your daily tasks. Why don't you start with an easy one? Write down your daily mantra at the top of today's page. Write it down and reference it at least three times today; ideally when your resolve is floundering.

Getting in

*'If Tetris teaches us anything, it is that fitting
in will cause you to disappear. Be unique'*

Dress appropriately – it's not leg day

The time has come; you've done the necessary back-end graft
to ensure you get in the door and get the opportunity to 'sell
yourself'. Remember, life is a sales pitch. You sell yourself all the
time: to your clients, in an interview or to your potential partner
and, obviously, when you sell a product. Some people even need
to sell themselves to *themselves*, just to make sure they believe
in their own self-image.

First impressions are vital and unfortunately they can be the
things that make or break your interview, when it comes to many
hiring managers; so it is best to play it safe and dress "smart".
Not a suit but trousers and a shirt with shoes; not a short skirt
or a deep neckline but a sensible blouse and skirt or trousers. No
sneakers, no singlets and no egos. You are not going to the gym
for leg day; you are going to a business to sell your services. If
you were going in to sell a financial product to a fitness company,
would you wear shorts and a t-shirt? No, so why would you do
it when you are selling yourself. The way you present yourself
sets the tone for the next step in the process – it's too casual, it
says you don't see this as a business. Always dress smart unless it
is otherwise specified; there *are* some locations where they may

request fitness attire if you are going to be doing some sort of practical training or such. However, this is rare.

Some companies will offer recruitment evenings where you'll have to interact with other applicants in a group setting. Some of these people may decide to come in casual gear but don't let this put *you* off. In fact, you'll stand out for the right reasons. When I was a hiring manager, I can't tell you how many times I had people arrive in an unprofessional manner and in inappropriate clothing, but it was too many times! Generally speaking those people showed a lack of care in their preparation for the interview in every sense, not just the dress code.

You want to ensure that you stand out from the crowd and that you are the person that is remembered. You do that by preparing properly and by not being late or tardy. Preparation is the key to a good first impression, in this climate you have no excuse not to prepare. You should be able to find out what your interviewer looks like, what makes them tick, what the company values are and what the job entails, as a minimum, prior to attending any interview. As you will see in the next section, the interviewer will be prepared with a backstory of you as well as what they want, so know what they want and why.

Challenge

First impressions, you only get one chance.

Try to put this to the test in your own life. Challenge yourself to dress smartly at all times, as best you can. You never know when an opportunity will knock and generally speaking it knocks first at the doors of those who are dressed and ready for work. Dress for the job you want, not the job you have!

Trust me, we will scope you out

A lot of hiring managers I know will have already sussed you out, through LinkedIn before your interview day or your fitness industry recruitment evening.

If you don't have a LinkedIn account and you're reading this, please get one. Its free, it's easy and it can open doors and opportunities for you further down the track. I have actively recruited from there. It has also given me the opportunity to verify what people say in their interviews. It is a great communication tool and a good way to create business networks further on, but we'll get to that later on in the section on social media.

It doesn't just stop there. Some people will check out your LinkedIn entry to see the professional side of you before moving on to the 'not so professional' side which can be accessed through Facebook and other similar sites. Make sure that before you start the application process, you tidy up your social accounts. If you're aiming to become a PT at a prestigious studio, your promotion of alcoholism isn't the best sales tool for you right now, is it? Right or wrong, some people will actively look at your social media sites beforehand and will make assumptions about you based on the information they find there. Do yourself a favour, give people less ammo to use against you and give yourself every chance you can get!

OK, some of you might argue that your accounts are yours and you are free to post whatever it is you like. Just remember that perhaps you friended your boss on-line and he/she can see your profile too. Does that make things awkward?

Never publicise your disdain for a member, for a colleague or for your manager for that matter - you have seen all those horror stories about where an employee has faced disciplinary action for something similar. These days, most companies have a social media policy and there is a strong likelihood that if you post something offensive or work-related it can come back to haunt you. As my grandmother always said to me, as a young lad, 'if you don't have anything nice to say, then don't say anything at all'. I don't want to see any memes on your page which show how disappointed you are with such and such or how your employer is not treating you right. Take that up with your employer directly, not through a public forum where everyone can see how you think out loud. As I mentioned earlier, you may bad mouth one company today and that comment may follow you around for some time. Don't be a victim of online awkwardness, just let common sense prevail.

Remember you are aiming to get involved in the fitness industry now. It's a well-connected, closely knit and very social bunch with access to modern technologies. Any ill behaviour will spread quickly. Please don't become the next viral trend; at least not for the wrong reasons.

Challenge

Go through your social media accounts today. Look at and think about how they make you look. If the answer is 'not professional' or something similar then make them private, hide them, delete them; whatever does the trick. It is an interesting exercise to write down how many pictures or comments you had to delete, at the end of this. Trust me, it is very interesting. I want you to be strong in this section; view it through the eyes of your parish priest, your mother and your boss all in one!

Do your homework

Preparation is also vital in this game; you need to ensure that you are ready for all the questions that will come at you as well as understanding the expectations that are the norm in the industry.

Personal trainers, membership consultants, management: is there some overtime required? Definitely. If you want to succeed in this industry, it's non-negotiable, a bare minimum, a requirement. However, there are not many who are willing to do this and for this reason those who *are* willing will generally push themselves forward, up the corporate ladder, at a very fast pace.

Know this: long hours are the norm; so, if you are asked about your availability, say *'every day'*, just in case.

Take the time to find out something about the business itself. Learn everything you can about them before you meet them. Google can be your best friend, the week before. Find out how many locations they have. Make sure you have already visited at least one before the interview to get an idea of what they offer. Can you list their core values and incorporate them into your answers? I would say that all of these points are the bare minimum of requirements.

Fail to prepare and you prepare to fail. This is something I truly believe; make sure that you have completed your due diligence on the business before you take the opportunity to sell yourself. Is it a small boutique site, a new site, a small owner operator? Can you find out about the owner or the investor(s)? Can you find out about their membership base?

The types of organisations vary greatly and therefore so do their requirements. As an example, is it a PLC, a large scale organisation who has investors? Companies such as this are generally very heavily focused on KPIs and their main aim is running a profitable business. By the way, now might be a good time to mention that if you are opening your own business, this is actually a pretty good strategy to take on board. A rural fitness centre is something completely different. Normally this is an environment that offers a purely service-based product. It aims to ensure the community are made to feel included and it promotes a healthy lifestyle. These two examples of different types of facilities will both have very different ideas of what the job calls for in each location.

All of this research gets you valuable background information for your interview and it also shows that you have the resources to find information and to work autonomously with self direction. In other words, this shows preparation.

Challenge

Decide what type of business you want to work in/with today or where you want to work tomorrow. Is it a large MNC, a franchise, a small boutique gym, a health club or a government facility? The list is endless and there are pros and cons that can be made for each option. Once again, decide what works for you. Maybe you want to open your own facility, to run your own small business or to operate externally as a contractor. Whatever your goal is, use the sections that follow to help you decide and make a choice for yourself.

You're in

It's not all Yoga and push ups

Small industry

The fitness industry is a close-knit community where everyone and, trust me I mean *everyone*, knows one another! My biggest piece of advice to you is never go out on your back, always go out on your shield. Time and time again I have seen cases where people think they are done with a position and just give up. Their work ethic drops and unfortunately that is the lasting image that remains in people's heads. Don't be that person.

A quick look at the industry will show you that there are a few key players, larger organisations, who have a big say in the industry and who are also are very well connected. Staff from different brands meet up together and connect, chatting about the job regularly. It pays to be loyal to the industry and to yourself rather than trying to stay loyal to just one brand. Don't ever do something that might tarnish your personal reputation, i.e. don't talk down a competitor - you never know when you might be asking them for a job! I am speaking from experience; I know this happens. While I am on this subject; here's a top tip for you hiring managers out there. When you are calling the reference checks on a candidate's resume, if it seems in anyway suspect then I recommend you call the facility or club where the candidate says/said they work(ed). The general manager there is usually a good person to ask about that person's character.

You would be amazed to hear some of the horror stories I have heard - when someone spoke to someone else's best mate who was pretending to be his line manager - they have put me off making silly hiring mistakes.

All your varied work experiences give you different skillsets no matter where you have worked: a small owner operator site, a franchise or a large scale corporation. They all provide you with opportunities to learn and it is actually a good idea to chop and change between the various types and sizes of facilities. You'll get good experience of what it is like in a particular setting and in this way you'll build up a bigger and better version of you and your personal business.

So, remember the fitness industry is well connected. It's very social, very vocal and nothing is forgotten. Do right by your current employer; by the one you are going to work for next and the one you would like to work for. Don't ever leave on bad terms; who knows when it will come back to bite you. Oh, and a word to you managers out there: don't ever adopt the stick approach. It's the same for you; you never know when the tables may be turned and one of your direct reports may be managing you one day!

So, what does this all mean? How do you interact and operate in such an environment? Well, it's simple. Just focus on one key word: integrity. Have integrity about the way you carry and conduct yourself. Yes, it might be really easy to leave a PT contract mid-term and to jump ship (if you are at all good in dissecting a contract) however; you may be doing irreparable damage to your personal reputation. What's worse you may never get work within a 50 km radius of that facility, ever again. It's just not worth it!

Challenge

Define what your version of integrity is? What does it mean to you? Please write the answers below.

I'll tell you what it is for me. It is doing the right thing, all the time. That means doing the right thing when it's the easy way to do the right thing but more importantly when it's the hard option!

What is it to you?

_____

_____

_____

_____

_____

ABN/TFN

Now let's get into the nitty gritty. Do you want to do work for yourself? Do you maybe want to work for someone else? There are pros and cons to both of these options but for the moment it is important to understand what they both entail and how this can affect you.

Being an ABN (Australian Business Number) contractor means that you are entitled to run your own business (sometimes inside a facility), in any way that you would like to and on your terms. Essentially you get to be your own boss; great isn't it. Well, yes it is, if you are ready for the responsibilities that come along with it. You need to understand that you don't get annual leave payments, you don't automatically receive superannuation and you don't automatically get taxed. In fact you need to organise all your tax payments yourself and this is a point where a lot of new PTs fall down. You should be prepared for everything that is expected of you when you are an ABN trainer or other role. It can be very challenging and stressful but it can also be extremely rewarding, if you do it right. My fiancée is a PT by trade. She works for herself and she loves it. However, I have seen at least fifty others come through the doors that were not able to get past the first couple of months; for some people it is simply too much too early. It is free to get an ABN through the Australian government website. It takes little preparation to apply and get it, yet it also takes a huge amount of preparation to run a business properly. Please make sure you know what you are getting yourself into.

A lot of new graduates from the fitness education institutes are extremely eager to get involved but don't have an iota of what it actually entails. To me, this shows a serious lack of clarity which needs to be corrected and which I will do my best to address in the following pages. Yes, it *is* exciting; yes, there is the promise of a large earning capacity for a small investment of time. But, and this is the key, this is all only available if you know what you're talking about and if you understand how to first plan for business. If a SWOT analysis, a business plan, the four P's of marketing or any other basic business terms aren't in your knowledge base, then I suggest you hold off on any movement until you get your skills up to scratch.

I hate to cite examples which scared me but the following one did; it really made me look at the industry through a different set of goggles and it made me look at the industry for what it really was: an industry full of lions and gazelles. Lions wake up on Monday morning and they know they are a lion; they never second guess that fact, they never worry about their strength or their power, they are comfortable in their position in the jungle: Some trainers need to be more like lions. Lions don't wake up on a Monday morning complaining about being tired, they go around eating things as normal and if you step into their domain they eat you too! Know what you are and what you are not. I once had a poor chap apply for a position to become a personal trainer: an ABN trainer operating out of a facility which I was in charge of. I asked him one simple question, where do you see yourself, session-wise, in three months' time once the full rent has kicked in. At that time the full rent at the facility was roughly three hundred dollars a week. He said he wanted to have at least five paid sessions by then. I couldn't believe what I was hearing. He had pretty much said that he wanted to be losing fifty dollars a week as his goal in three months' time. I say the poor chap because he simply didn't quite get it. I actually felt for him and gave him some advice which I hope he followed up on. I advised that he should find out why he wants to be a trainer; he should do a business course and if at that stage he still wants to be a personal trainer come back and talk to me. He hasn't come back yet and I doubt he will cross my path any time soon. Don't be a gazelle, be a lion.

On the other hand, working for someone also has its "wins" and "losses". Some of the wins include: superannuation, paid sick leave, annual leave, commissions, salary and stability. It is also a bit easier to get a loan and/or mortgage, if your salary is high enough. However, in the short term it does also limit your capacity for earnings, to some degree (unless a role with commission comes up, which we will discuss a little later on). It really just boils down to what you value more and what line of work you are looking to get into. Most people in sales/management prefer to work for someone, unless they have opened their own studio/facility/site, whereas these days, a lot of trainers work for themselves and sub-contract their services to facilities. Of course, there are also sales people who run sales businesses and who sub-contract their services to vendors on a short/long term basis.

Look at both options critically and see if you are ready to make a decision about what works best in your current situation and personal circumstances.

Challenge

Study the taxation chart and armed with this knowledge work out how much you would have to pay on your desired earnings? As an example, if you want gross earnings of $150,000 a year, how much would you be taxed as an individual and how much would you need to pay as a business?

I want you all to source a good accountant, today. Look for one who is based as locally as possible and who has worked with fitness industry staff before. You should also begin to document any work related expenses and to jot them down (if you haven't already started this). Keep receipts and start a storage system for them. Keep them all year until tax return time. This can be a real money saver in the long run. Yes, it can be annoying at first, but it will become second nature after you've seen how much money you can save!

Commissioned heavily

A common phrase you will see/hear in the fitness industry is OTE. This stands for on target earnings, which means it is what you could receive if you worked like a winner. It's an interesting concept: working like a winner. It is something I truly believe in and it can totally make or break a good industry rep. We've all heard the sayings, but in my opinion the world is the way you see it. If you see a lot of clouds well don't be surprised when it starts pissing down rain; choose to see sunshine and you will get a tan! This belief needs to be the cornerstone of your being, if you are going to get involved in this industry. Whether you are a success or a failure can very quickly depend on your attitude. Your attitude can affect you big time in a commissioned role, so it's up to you not to let it be the deciding factor in your fate.

I hear you asking, *"What is commission and how does it work?"* Well, essentially it is a payment for doing well and in many fitness industry roles it is 'uncapped'. This means that you can earn an exponential amount of income just in pure commission and that's on top of your base salary. Cha-ching! How great is that? The opportunity to earn more; it's like you can basically set your own salary, even as an employee! Who wouldn't love that? It turns out that there's rather a lot of people who wouldn't.

I have heard all that salary/work balance talk before. 'I really want to work in this industry but I have been offered a job in a city-based office for $3 more per hour'. My answer is, *"Are you mad?"* You are giving up before you have even started. If you're not willing to work for your money, then I wouldn't want to hire you and neither would many other companies. If you want extra money you have to be willing to work extra hours. An entry level sales consultant can earn anywhere between the start of the $30,000s to well above $100,000 per annum. So it's possible to be more than three times more successful than the next person... But why is this and how can I do this? You ask. Well, it's not rocket science. How do you do it? By working. By working every day you are rostered to work and by actually being there. By arriving at work and actually being present. By being ON where you are in.

When I started in sales, in the fitness industry, my salary was extremely low, however after I had moved from Ireland to Australia; it didn't really seem as low, at that time, as some others saw it. You know, the only thing I remember from my interview was the word 'uncapped'. The commission was uncapped. Sign me up, I remember thinking to myself. That first month in the sales room I made double my salary in commissions alone! It can be done, but only if you turn up every day and *make an effort!*

Don't get scared, get involved. Tough it out. A great added advantage is that as you prove yourself in these arenas, you not only move up the ranks but you also learn valuable sales skills along the way. I thoroughly recommend sales as a great entry point for everyone and all tasks in the industry.

Too often these days, people chop and change between industries and companies as quickly as they change their minds. Millennials are especially known for job-hopping and this is evident on most of the resumes you'll see these days: six months at this company, a year at that, before changing industries. In my opinion there is something to be said for good old fashioned graft and toughing it out to work your way up. I often use the analogy of an Olympic sportsperson: a boxer has to train for at least four to eight years before they get their big break into the Olympic scene. They try to keep consistent with coaching and everything around them; they show up every day for four to eight years to compete for three minutes a round. You don't see a boxer trying his or her hand at the equestrian events or sprinting; you don't see them going from one trainer to another. You see consistent effort. There is something to be said for this approach: These days we are too hasty in our expectations, hoping to become a CEO overnight. The saying that overnight success takes ten years is very true. So, to all of you out there who are struggling in your first month and wanting to pack it in, think of this Olympic analogy. To be a great success you must first make great sacrifices, every day, for years.

Show up every day for at least four years. If after that time you don't learn or do enough to make your move, then you can review.

Challenge

Let's bring the subject back to goal setting with a financial goal breakdown. If you have a certain financial figure in mind that you want to hit for your yearly earnings, then find out how many sales per week or how many clients per week or whatever it is you need to do or sell to create that income level that you're chasing. At the top end in sales some companies pay up to $50 per sale; can you sell 100 memberships in a month? If so that is $5'000 extra just from commission. Get thinking about your financial goal; get calculating and start earning!

Systems use

*'Manage numbers,
lead people'*

Prospecting systems that work

If this doesn't make sense to start with at this stage, that's ok, but very soon you will need to understand how and what is explained in this section about prospecting, because this is the make and break point for you and your business. Prospects are everywhere you just need to capture them. The mantra of ABC (Always be closing) needs to be stuck in your head as you walk through the world of prospects. We will look at some of the ways in which you gather data about leads later on in the next chapter, but now let's talk concepts. Let's talk about how you can prospect and track, via systems use.

You'll find that most large membership businesses will use a prospect system, such as Gymsales or InTouch or similar. Some even have their own internally designed systems. Information systems make your job so much easier; it means easy tracking and data analysis and that lets you spend your time on what is important which is building your business. A good prospect systematic plan is; track, review and move forward.

Track – Track all opportunities that you may receive on a daily basis. You must ensure you capture the necessary data for follow up. Without follow up you are simply another membership business, lost in translation, amongst all of the marketing collateral and advertising with which modern society is awash. You want to be the one that stands out with the human touch, the follow up. You need to offer the personalised response; the magic of humanity.

Review – Once you have captured your valuable data, then you can trail back over those results and see what types of data you have got and decide what success you are then having with that data. Is there a particular group, segment or demographic that you are currently having clear successes with? If so, ensure you maximise this and continue working a good resource. If however, you notice that you are performing poorly with another segment, then you may need to look for methods to improve communication with this group. If you notice, for example, that the males aged 20-30 demographic is performing poorly, ask yourself if you could perhaps include more targeted imagery to suit this market. Look at edgy, sporty and 'tough' styled marketing follow-ups.

Move Forward – Continue on the process. You have captured all of the necessary data via a prospecting system; you have then reviewed the success/failure of certain capture and followed up. Use the learning from the review section to help implement change in your staff training. It could be that your telephone sales' team need to understand that when talking to a market of female 50-65 year olds they might need to change their tone to suit the audience. Where you may have previously asked them to really pump up the volume and be super enthusiastic, you may discover that a tone adjustment may be required to ensure success with this particular demographic.

Generally, when I speak about prospecting information systems what you want is to extrapolate key data from prospects. Three key items of information might be their *name, phone number and email address.* All of these can be used to your advantage in phone scripting, sales pitches and beyond. At a bare minimum you will need to capture names and at least one contact method; otherwise there is no point in handing out free passes, or free sessions or even giving them your business card. You may as well wipe your hands clean of them in 99% of the cases, if you don't have that most basic of information. So, remember, it is crucial to grab their details so you can follow up. No follow up; no sale!

Challenge

Prospecting is like looking for gold in an area where you think there may be potential. Right now, I want you to think of one key area you haven't looked at before and see if that could be a viable area to gather prospect data from. I'll start you off with an example. When I started out I didn't realise that the local chamber of commerce was an area that I could go into and network through in order to gain heaps of business leads. Do you have a local chamber of commerce or something similar where you can prospect?

Manual tracking sheets

Whatever the sales process you are involved in, be it selling your PT services, selling memberships or selling a business, you will need to make sure that you capture more data whenever you get the opportunity to do so. A guest register is a great start and it's a great tool to have in your membership business. If you don't have one today; then make one, quickly. It is a something you can use to capture the details from non-members such as name, number, email, time of visit, reasons for visit, signature, emergency contact etc. However, like a lot of tools, it's only great when it's used correctly. My advice to you is to fill it in with black pen in clear text, when you come in first thing in the morning. In the space for "Reason for Visit", write 'to join the special deal' or something similar. What you'll find is that once one person writes down reason for visit as this or a 'free pass' then everyone below them will do the same. Most people want to be like most other people. Make sure that you are watching as they fill in the form so that you can be sure that they have included all sections. It's also a useful opportunity to do a meet and greet. This should be monitored by your sales team and *not* the reception team, if you have both. The reason for this is that if the sales team is commissioned for sales they will see every opportunity as gold and will treat it accordingly. At every interaction they will be striving to sell subtly and with a different sense of urgency. The same applies to your PT consults, especially the free ones. These can generate leads for potential new clients. You will still need to capture all of the above details, as well as starting to establish a personal relationship and to go into a detailed needs analysis.

The aim of this document is to make it an easy tool to integrate into any other systems you may already have. Your manual tracking sheets may be automated directly from contact one, if you have the spending power to ensure that all prospects/guests are able to enter their details via an online portal/app check-in or similar. The world is your oyster; just make sure that you have some form of key-data capture in your entry way. The only real issue with the manual process is that it does open you up to human error: poor clarity in handwriting is commonplace and if the amount of data is large it can cause double handling because of data entry, after the fact. In an ideal world this data should either be entered as you go or entered directly into a system which 'plugs in' to your business intelligence system.

It is also always good to have a manual system, as a back-up – because when I.T products go down, and yes unfortunately at times they will go down, you do not want to be caught short. Ensure you have a backup process and procedure for 'systems down' time with manual paperwork that you can follow.

Challenge

Go and workout casually at a local fitness centre and see what type of guest register system they have in place; the scary thing is a lot of them have no type of data capturing system at all. If they do have one, dissect it as you fill it in and see what you could improve for you or your business. Remember that if you have had to pay for this visit, then get a tax receipt as discussed in previous chapters! This is a work-related expense, research!

Data analysis

Data analysis is all about graphs, charts, images and all that fun stuff. It is great to see your statistical data displayed in a graph format because it lets you easily see where you are doing well and what you are doing poorly. It is also the easiest and quickest way to see what you might do differently.

Most modern systems can explain to you where you are gathering the bulk of your prospects from in detail and can tell you what data is missing that you should be capturing. The systems that you have at your fingertips these days are so advanced that, frankly, it would be a shame *not* to use them. My advice to you is to make sure that you get comfortable with technology because as of right now it can be a massive help to you and your business.

With just a little bit of "techy" know-how and by being up to speed with current tech advancements, you can remain in the loop and will understand how you can use technology for and in your business.

There are also some great business data analysis apps, one great app I use and it is free is 'Facebook pages'. It focuses on your business Facebook page and gives you some great statistical analysis. Budget spreadsheets, such as YNAB (You need a budget) are also great and can serve as a visual reminder and as an aid to recording and tracking expenditure. Finally, you have tools such as apps for keeping receipts where you can track your receipts in and section them off into different spending areas. This is just one of many areas where you can get up close and personal with your data. Many PTs out there also use a debiting system such as EZDebit, Debit Success or various other debiting companies. Make sure that you make use of the reporting and statistics sections; once you've played with this a few times and got an understanding of what it does, you'll never look back.

Challenge

Download all of the apps I just mentioned (they are free) and get a basic knowledge of how they operate, then start to incorporate them into your daily routine.

Lead Generation

Everyone is a lead if you think they are;
don't narrow your search
before you've even begun.

Get out to get business in

Lead generation is the main area where the good are separated from the great. If you can generate leads effectively, you will guarantee your business success once your product offering is strong. However, you have to get out of your comfort zone if you want to achieve lead generation success. It can be uncomfortable and confronting initially, especially if you don't have a sales background. Another thing I have to mention is that it might not sit well with your morals as it were at first. However, don't think about it as selling product per se. You need to understand that what you are doing is offering people a chance to improve their health and fitness. That really is the best product you can ever offer someone; you literally have an opportunity to save lives. This is the reason that I will continue to push health and fitness until I am blue in the face! But before you can sell it to anyone else, you have to first sell yourself.

Try to think of this process as a learning curve where you have to throw yourself into the deep end as soon as you are able. Lead generation is the starting point for the sales funnel process; it's the activator at the beginning that increases sales' results at the back-end.

You might get sales initially because you're new and different, without having a proactive lead generation process in place, but this industry moves quickly and you will only be new or different for so long. Before you know it you will be a 'me too' business and you will risk stagnating and seeing your sales funnel dry up. Before this happens you need to think proactively and start to push people into your sales funnel from the top down.

You are now a brand evangelist for you and your business. If you have this in mind during every interaction, you will find that you are adhering to the principle of always be closing (ABC) automatically. Make sure that you get the chance to preach about what you do, at every opportunity. A brand evangelist spreads the good word about their fitness business, in much the same way as the apostles spread the good word of God. No joke; you will be preaching about changing and improving lives through fitness and good health!

Remember you need to always be on; essentially, you are on the campaign trail like a politician coming up to an election, but you are in a perpetual campaign state. You need to be the face of the business: shake hands, wave, kiss the babies and smile for photos just like a politician would. In fact, the only difference between you and a politician in this lead generation state, is that they are trying to get a vote and you are trying to get new business.

If done correctly, lead generation has a dual approach: what we call Business to Customer (B2C) (quick results) and Business to Business (B2B) (longer and slower but with bigger results). You need to have a mixture of the two in your lead generation strategy, with 70% focus aimed towards the B2C market and 30% geared at B2B. This may differ slightly depending on your product offerings. As an example, if you offer corporate fitness for the mining industry then your B2B percentage would be more heavily weighted.

There are numerous ways to foster lead generation. Before we discuss the power of B2B below, think about networking and the simple power of saying *"hello"*. I'll also list some other clever ways of doing lead generation and you can see if any of them would fit in with your business model.

Lead boxes – (for example, a 'win big' entrance box where your prospect enters their details to win a free pass, a free PT session, a free etc.…). You get the drift. In this case one person wins the big prize but everyone else wins the secondary prize - a free 'lesser value product' e.g. a free health consult. This is a tool for generating leads. Get these boxes designed professionally and get as many out as you can.

Social media and on-line; we'll discuss these again in more detail later, but suffice to say at this stage that you can base your strategies around Likes and Shares, promotions with prizes and 'content based' activities.

Outreach – this is getting out to get business in. It's the fun campaigns that entice people into your business. It's roaming lead generation activities.

Casual leasing – book a site in a mall or similar to sell your wares and promote your business.

Health surveys – you can use these to capture lead data and also to subtly set a prospect up for success. You can ask questions, such as how important is fitness to you, do you monitor your diet etc. and at the end you offer them an opportunity to get a free entry based on their responses. This is a very clever strategy to extrapolate lead data from prospects.

Partnerships with other organisations in a similar space can complement your product offering, e.g. imagine an expensive corporate fitness centre where a lot of member's drive fancy German cars, if there was a high level car wash nearby, it would be a great blend to offer a deal between the two of you. Think of ways this can work for you.

In reach – Point of sale referrals - this is getting business from your current clientele. It's a huge opportunity that is often neglected. It's actually one of the best ways to gain leads, and not just any lead but hot solid leads. But hold that thought for a little while; we'll delve into this further in the referral chapter.

E content – email out content to try to get business in. Once again there are some simple actions you can take today that will increase your 'e-approach'. For example, even your email signature gives you an opportunity to sell to the people who receive your emails. If you don't have one then add one, now. In it you can create a call to action. It can slot in under your signature. An example could be:

"Regards,

Shane McKeogh

Click HERE for a VIP FITNESS PASS."

Ensure you are selling in your email signature, as much as you are in a sales presentation, by simply tweaking the small "one percenters".

Now that you have looked at some of the options which are available to you for capturing leads, you need to look at what attributes or skills you might need in order to capture real leads in real time.

There are three keys to being a lead generation superstar; back yourself (be confident), no is just a 'W' away from now and, lastly, everyone deserves a shot.

Back yourself – if you don't have confidence in the lead generation process you will not come across with integrity, and you will sound suspect because you are unsure of yourself. Don't let *you* become your biggest problem. Once, whilst training a team of salespeople how to gather mass leads in minimum time, I showed them how I do it, live in front of their eyes. However, I got feedback the following week where I was told that it has been unfair as I was clearly confident in the process and obviously I could do it with ease because of that. My response to them was simple - then you need to be confident. Now, this same team is well able to gather the right type of and the right number of leads, because they are coming from a point of confidence.

No is just a 'W' away from now – the words no and now are separated by one little 'w'. To get to the point where you want to be, that is the 'now', you must first achieve countless No's. I say *achieve* a no because that is what you need to do. You need to view these as an accolade; guess what? I have managed to get ten No's. Great work, you are sure to get to the 'now' you want soon. Never be disheartened by a 'no'. Always take it and deal with it as you move forward to your 'now' goal. Ironically, as I sit here in the 'W' resort in Bali, I feel as though this may be creeping into my writing, as I am staring at a giant 'W' sign for the resort!

Everyone deserves a shot – ask everyone, every day. No one person should be asked for their lead details over another: If you follow the simple rule of asking every one you will avoid isolating anyone and letting any personal bias enter your mind. A story, which I saw unfold right before my eyes, showed me how not asking someone can actually upset that person, even though you thought you were doing the right thing. I had a team of street representatives trying to sign people up to a new gym that was opening. The team was located on a casual leasing stand in a shopping centre and were having a slow day. You already know I am brazen and always back myself, as per my previous point. So with that in mind, I went to visit the site to see how the day was going and I saw the team seemed disheartened; they seemed down. They told me it was too hard, it was too difficult and too everything else. You name it; they blamed the poor performance on that. Basically they were being gazelles not lions. So in the spirit of backing myself I said, *"put five minutes on the clock and I will get a sale, guaranteed"*. I walked into the nearest shop to ask a woman there if she had heard about our business and I was astonished by her reply. This great lady was clearly in need of some fitness help and was, by her own admission, obese. She said she walked past the casual leasing stand three times that day in the hope that the team would offer her some information on how to join, yet they didn't because they thought if they asked her they would offend her. Ironically, in her mind she thought they didn't ask her because she didn't look like a gym person. So in essence by not asking this person they had made her feel worse about herself. This conversation lasted five minutes and she was sold. I backed myself and, better still, I made a woman feel comfortable again explaining what we would do to help her move forward. This team now ask everyone, every day.

Believe me there are so many ways to generate leads I could write a book on lead generation, alone. Maybe I will do - keep your eyes peeled!

Challenge

Organise *your* lead generation strategy and make sure you target one option in each section. Plan your lead generation strategy out today and follow up with at least one area per week until you have completed all eight sections:

1. Lead Box

2. Social Media

3. Outreach

4. Casual Leasing

5. Health Survey

6. Partnerships

7. In reach

8. E-content

Once you have completed them and decided what you will do, then simply go ahead and do that.

B2B networking

Business to Business (B2B) is an approach where you deal with a business entity first and foremost rather than an individual. However, you will quickly find that B2B is essentially Business to Customer (B2C) on a grander scale as you are still doing business with people. This process revolves around selling your business proposition to another business, generally under the premise of what can you do for one another or how can you establish a mutually beneficial agreement where both parties see some wins.

Writing about this takes me back to a B2B partnership I set up with a local sports' team. It was an ice hockey team in fact - not an overly popular sport in Australia, as you can imagine with the weather! The team was called Perth Thunder and what they wanted was an opportunity to reach more fans. What better way than to access our database of 30'000 plus members in Western Australia alone. For us it was an opportunity to attend games, to get permanent signage in an ice hockey rink and to become the fitness partner of the players themselves. We counted on the fans following what their favourite sports stars did. It took a couple of meetings to set this up followed by a letter of intent and a contract which was drawn up and edited until we were both happy and then an agreement was reached between the two companies.

In fact, networking really is an easy process. All it really means is reaching out to businesses on a daily basis and seeing who gets back to you. You are still doing lead generation, just on a bigger scale. It is crucial that there is a good 'link' between the companies and that it is a good 'fit' for both parties, e.g. partnering with a health-food store is a better idea than partnering with a take away restaurant which sells cakes. Once again the link is clearly stronger with the "healthy business".

Don't forget the smaller scale opportunities; local businesses can be your first ports of call. This has many advantages, small scale owner-operators and SMES (Small medium size enterprises) have more flexibility in what they can and cannot do. Large multinational corporations (MNC's) need to jump through hoops and get approval at many different levels which means the acceptance process is dragged out and you have to spend a lot of time on them. Another advantage to working local is that you can sell this as a USP (Unique Selling Point). You can point out that you and your business work with local vendors and this in turn can get you the buy-in that you so desperately seek from the local community.

Yes, the large national and international companies are great and they can yield massive results. You would be surprised what a quick email or a call can do. I recently met with a large mining company, on a whim and managed to establish a partnership for our company which gives us access to over 2000 employees. That is 2000 more eyes on our product offerings and if we can translate this into dollars then it was certainly a huge win.

Design a corporate listing of who you have already spoken with, what they want and what you can offer to them. Once again the initial aim of the game is to grab lead details i.e. the best contact point for the owner/manager, email address, contact number and what they want. Then from here you can continue to touch base with them and ensure you follow up accordingly. If you have a team working for you, make sure they all have a section to follow up and that they don't cross over. That would mean that in a team of four, for example, you could divide the sections up by postcode, or a km radius to be certain that you are not all offering the same product to the same people. See an example of a corporate lead template, in the challenge section of this chapter.

The B2B process is a fun one to be involved with and usually involves a lot of coffee, meetings and similar. It can also be stressful and intimidating if you are not prepared for, or versed in, modern business practices. Get used to meeting people you have never met before and pitching your business in a light that shows how partnering with you can be of benefit to you both. The question people often ask themselves is: "What's in it for me?"(WIIFM). Simply design a pitch that shows them what is in it for them. Then you are not selling, you are merely showing the other business how you can both achieve success, whilst working hand in hand to foster links between both businesses that can yield future results down the track. Think outside the box; which people can you approach and in what fashion can you approach them? Say you run a massage business, for example, can you link up with any other allied health professionals to create a joint business offering for a particular period of time? Can you work with other allied health professionals in your local area to organise a local health and wellness event to increase foot traffic to the area and hopefully to use both health services? You do not need to compete - you can connect.

The business marketplace today is definitely open 24/7, so make sure that you get involved in this sector. It is laden with opportunities to be captured by the best in class. All it takes is an opportunistic mind-set and some grit to get the meeting. Once you get the meeting and demonstrate the right mutually beneficial scenario for all involved, it is pretty easy to close. You would probably also be surprised at what you can get for free, or as part of a contra-element, of the contract. Aim to get free 'win-wins' first, then look at contra-elements you can throw in to sweeten the deal. If you are a health club business, then you could talk contra-elements in terms of membership value. The other business may be chasing a ten-thousand-dollar investment and you counter offer with contra terms such as ten memberships valued at eight thousand dollars and an extra two thousand dollars' value in club marketing. Thus, you are spending zero dollars of monetary funds; you are only spending in non-monetary terms. The only caveat here is to make sure that there is not too much 'debt' surrounding the company, i.e. don't overpromise and partner with everyone based on contra-elements because what will happen if all of the one hundred companies you partner with take you up on those memberships. Can you meet demand? If so great, if not be cautious. Think about your business offering and what you can add to a contract as a contra element.

In this case you need to look at the potential upshot of partnering with another company and what tangibles you might receive from this partnership. What is the return on investment (ROI) and what are the intangibles of this partnership such as brand awareness and business representation in new markets? Can you put a total tangible figure on what this partnership is worth to you?

Challenge

Fill in your corporate lead template. Fill in at least five business partners who you could potentially team up with to ensure a mutual win for you both. Design a quick two-minute pitch for each and think about how you would 'sell' to each of them. Remember you can get this for *free* if you offer the right product. Perhaps you could offer a membership term or training sessions instead of a straight dollar value. They may ask for a financial buy in but you can respond with a 'non-monetary' option which ensures your B2B strategy is not costing you too much money.

Fill in template on next page:

Design a list of local owner-operator businesses that fit into your version of the 'fitmosphere' and then establish a contact point and plan of attack for each company.

CORPORATE LEAD TEMPLATE: EXAMPLE ONE

Business Name	Business Industry	Staff #s?	What can we do for them?	What do they want from us?	Manager/ Owner name	Email Address	Phone No.
Welsas Foods	Health Food	500+	Advertise, cross promotion, Employee benefits package	Advertising, access to database, fitness seminars,	Paul Williams CEO	Paulwilliams@ welsasfoods. com.au OR Sales@ welsasfoods. com.au	0406... OR 08...

The power of hello

You know, it seems very simple to me but when I ask membership consultants, managers and personal trainers *"Do you know what power 'hello' has?"*, they are all mystified.

This is something that I have implemented into my own lead generation approaches. When you walk from your office, your home or your facility to another location for whatever reason: to get a coffee, to get the mail etc. just see how many people you can say hello to. It's so simple, I'm really surprised no one does it. I try to say hello to fifteen people on my walk from my office to the coffee shop. Of those fifteen, generally two or three will stop for a chat and I could prospect one or two of those and then grab one or two more leads just while I am getting a coffee. I sometimes have five coffees a day! Do the maths, that's nearly ten leads a day from buying coffee. I know some of you probably think I should stop drinking coffee, but it is my only vice and also a great form of lead generation as you can see.

Does it seem super simple? That's because, hey it is, but we often don't do it. It is scary to say hello to someone you don't know and nowadays people sometimes look at you a bit strangely when you do; so be it. Get comfortable, being uncomfortable. When you are in the elevator, spark the conversation; don't just stare at your phone. You never know who you are standing next to. It could be a key player that you might like to get to know.

Too often in life we walk around with blinkers on, staring at our phones, scared to interact. We spend our time looking down at a screen rather than out into the world, and all the while missing potential human connections and opportunities. The next time you are in an elevator, use that time to connect not disconnect; you have a captive audience with nothing else to do but wait for their floor. See if you can softly open up the doors of communication - who knows where that might lead. When you are sitting at a bus stop every day with the same people, at the same time, say more than just hello. Segue into a conversation about how their day was, what they do, you just never know. I happened to stumble upon a great Facebook marketer whilst training at the gym; I bumped into a contracts' lawyer while in an elevator and plenty more. Eyes on the world, when you're in the world.

Just imagine what could have happened if you had only initiated a conversation with that person. That person could change your life; any person can. You may have been there before in your life: It could be someone who you fancy and would love to take out on a date or a potential business contact who you would love to connect with, but if you don't have the power to say hello nothing will ever transpire, that is for sure.

Remember you are brand evangelists now, so wherever you go, you preach about health and fitness and eventually you get followers. Here's another nice example; a personal trainer is getting her nails done in a nail salon and instead of talking she just gets on Facebook. What if they actually looked up and talked to the person in front of them. They might find out that the nail technician is getting married in six months. Slowly but surely, you start to bring in the fact that you are a PT and specialise in pre-wedding dress fitness, get fit for the wedding day/honeymoon beach trip or something similar. I think you might just have just uncovered a lead. This lead came from opening your eyes, talking to someone, saying hello and preaching about what you do.

'Hello' can be a scary word to utter to someone who you have never met or never even spoken to, but just think of the countless ways in which a conversation could go; what it could lead to and where it could take you. Many times, if you are wearing a uniform or branded attire, a prospect may bring up your business in conversation organically. In a sense, your public announcement of being in business is a conversation starter itself. This is where you may want to create a branded shirt or t-shirt for your business with a 'Follow me to 'insert gym name here'' for example, as a subtle selling tool. This is a great opportunity to work on building business in a casual setting. Just remember that people do business with people.

Say hello; it's not that hard.

Challenge

This is a fun one and it's also easy. Walk to the coffee shop (or whatever drink you are into – I don't know how anyone doesn't drink coffee these days, especially in the fitness industry with the hours we do!) and see how many people you can say hello to on your travels. Write that number down or remember it and the next time you do that trip try to increase that number. Continue to do this until you have got into the habit of saying hello to people you pass. When you are branded, i.e., in your uniform this is great advertising for your company because you are the face of the business and are being friendly, *'ipso facto'* your business must be friendly and inviting too.

Social Media

*Social butterflies out there;
this is your time to shine - turn your
extraversion into dollars!*

Engage and interact

Remember when we discussed you becoming a brand evangelist for your business? The same goes for on-line platforms where you need to be constant and current. If you're a fitness guru who sells healthy meals and programs, well then your online page should relate to that and should not have too much contradictory content. Of course you can use the tool for fun as well as relating to your members, clients and prospects but make sure you come across as engaging and not "salesy" on social media. There are so many avenues to pursue, Facebook, LinkedIn, Instagram, Pinterest, Snapchat and Twitter and these are just the first ones that come to my mind. I strongly advise that you understand the importance of being constant on these platforms; if you set up a business Instagram account link it to your Facebook page as well as other platforms because that makes posting content a simultaneous (and easier) process. It is pointless setting up a page and not posting, though many do this. Even if it is mostly free advertising that you are posting, remember, that you will actually be hurting your image if you post nothing at all.

Be who you are on-line and off. It is so common these days for people to portray a falsified image of themselves on social media. People see through that and they know that this is not the real you. People do business with people, so if you are going to be face-to-face with them at some point in your process, they need to know who the *real you* is.

An online presence is a minimum for any type of business today, and for one that wants to be current it is mandatory. It is a non-negotiable to be up to date with current trends and to ensure that you are speaking in the right tone for the format. Social media and online presence is not new and it has not crept up on us; yet some businesses seem to act as though it has snuck up on them in just the past few months. You must be as well versed with Snapchat as you are with a Profit and Loss account (P&L). This is because the leverage and correct marketing you get via snapchat, for example, could ultimately increase your revenue streams which thereafter impact your P&L's. Having business acumen in both historic business practices and skills with modern business tools are as important as one another and cannot be mutually exclusive. Do you know your Snapchat from your Twitter?

Set yourself up with numerous accounts and ensure you are across them all. These social media platforms are free, for the most part, and can be used with extreme success. The aim is to build a following (brand evangelists have followers, remember) and then nurture that group to become your own brand apostles who will spread the message of you and your business. It is not necessarily a sales pitch process but it will bring new business in its own way. The number of leads I receive on a daily basis through my Facebook business account is immense and I have sourced everything from personal trainers looking to pay rent at our facility, through new members wanting to join, to people wanting to get on board as employees. Be active and strong in using social media and it will return dividends in due time. The main thing here is to ensure that you focus on the right part for you. Most people think it is about how many followers they have and this may be true for certain business models, but for most it is about the engagement rate of your current followers that really matters. What is the use of having five hundred thousand uninterested followers if you sell protein powder in a bricks and mortar store? You would either need to create an online product, which you can leverage sales off, or focus on individuals in your location, who you can actually sell to and increase their average spend per purchase. So it isn't about the number of followers or fans you have but more their activity levels within your business. Think of what your business needs: activity within your business or purely mass coverage. What works for one may not work for another.

Challenge

Delete anything you would consider too sales-driven and increase the amount of content-driven posts, today.

Understand the expectations

How quickly you respond is crucial in social media, because it is so much more visible than the historic communication methods. Often someone may call a company to complain or send a letter; generally the people who know about this complaint are just the person complaining, maybe their friends and the business. However, nowadays if someone complains publicly online then it is just that: public - for all to see. For this reason we must understand and adapt to what we need to do to mitigate the risk of business exposure, but also to maximise this as an opportunity to respond and engage.

These days social is a great way to communicate but you need to understand that the expectations about responding are much different to those for an email or a letter. If you are going on a forum, you need to hold yourself accountable to their expectations not yours. Your antiquated expectations of a 48-hour turnaround time to respond are simply not good enough! You need to have a response time of less than two hours. Yes, this can become a serious work load issue, but you can automate responses as well as a lot of the processes, e.g. setting up scheduled posts etc.

I would recommend that if you have the man/woman power, get a staff member to become your social media guru and give them access and authority on the account. But don't forget to also give them some training on what is and isn't acceptable on social media. I have opened up access to some of my staff in the past and I have always got them to send me a draft of what they wanted to post before they actually did, as sometimes it would come across as sounding way too sales-driven, too pushy or sometimes just not relevant to the format. Through this, they learnt how to speak to a particular demographic in that particular format. Ironically some of these staff still send me messages prior to emailing and posting on social media, just to see what my thoughts are. Always do a couple of drafts before you send something! A lot can be lost in text and a lot can be taken out of context!

Challenge

Find out the norms in each of the following sites where you have a presence: LinkedIn, Facebook, Instagram, Twitter and Website. What time frames are people expecting to receive a response? What do those who are good on certain sites do on each site?

Can you improve upon your response time; can you link your accounts so that when you post on one you post on all, can you get a dedicated 'social media' staff member? All of these are great questions to consider and will help you set your definite social strategy

A new way to communicate

I want to reiterate that social media can be a really useful tool if you look at it as such. I will give you one prime example from my time in the sales room. When I landed in Western Australia from not-so-sunny Cork city in Ireland, you can well imagine that I didn't have much of a local lead database or a network. However, I did quickly realise that there was a large Irish community in Perth. So I searched on social media to see if there was a group where the Irish community could connect and quickly found such a group. In fact, I found many groups. My first task was to get online, get myself out there and ask. Initially my first month of business came from those groups and within that first month I made over seventy sales - much more than the top sales guys at the time. All of this happened in my first month, where at that stage I couldn't even speak proper 'Australian' and a lot of what I said was getting lost in translation. The motto of this story is to reach out and look at the different ways in which you can make social media work for you.

In a suburb, where one of our fitness centres was located we had a local community group page where we advertised some free fitness boot camps. These were given on the understanding that we were helping the local area get fitter (as we were not able to sell on this site) and from the attendance list at those boot camps we could take over with our sales process. Open your eyes and you will find many similar opportunities in your area and in your demographic.

Challenge

What can you do differently on social media? Can you source a new way of generating leads, a new sales tool or a new networking event?

Get on out and get active!

Sales – Big Revenue

*Either you run the day
or the day runs you*

It's a contact sport time to make some tackles

Good sales people know, that it is all about the contacts that you make and the more you make, the more opportunities you will have to become successful. Making tackles every day is how you win the game. Making contacts is the way that you get results consistently. Really, all you have to do in sales is make sure you show up day in and day out. Most great salespeople do one thing differently; even if they have a bad day, they do not let it affect the day after. They learn from it and get ready for the following day. You can always take the wins from a day but if you didn't get many sales on one day - ask yourself, if you were really focused on that or rather focused on booking up appointments for the next day and getting set up. Does your focus on getting new leads in your sales funnel ensure that you see results towards the end of the month? You choose how your day goes and even if it is going wrong, you still get to choose.

How many contacts should you make in a day? What is a contact?

A contact is an attempt to present your business to a current user or a potential user. It can be used to gain new business and to open up new business opportunities. How many calls can you make in a day to new business clients? Can you make twenty?

Brilliant! Set that as your goal. How many emails can you send to new business opportunities? Ten? How many social media responses or outgoing contacts can you make? How many face-to-face business opportunities can you present your business to?

If you sell fitness or health/wellness as a business and you want to be a success, then aim to make at least fifty contacts per day that are made up of the above methods of contact. Over the phone is key, in person is better and email, social media and B2B are all good ways to contact opportunities. There are so many.

If you can talk to fifty prospects in a day you *will* see tangible returns on this activity, if it is done correctly. If you know that what you are offering is needed and if you know how to sell it, you will do very well with that many contacts.

Picture a personal trainer who managed to contact fifty prospects in one day. Now, I know most trainers are busy during the times when people are able to answer their phones, however, it may be worth taking one day a month, or half a day a week that you can set aside purely for making outgoing calls and similar. In this way, you can ensure that you will stay busy and not just be busy for a short space of time. Keep your funnel full.

Think long term and increase your activity and contact methods to increase your sales revenue. Picking up the phone is not hard; it is not difficult to try something hard. It may be difficult to achieve success but only by trying will you increase your skill set. The more effort you make, the easier it becomes. Get on the phones early in the day to get a great start.

To achieve wild results, you must have a real key driver, a singular focus, a sense of purpose. With that in mind I use the acronym 'LASER' as a guide, to ensure my focus is constant and laser-like. So what is a 'LASER' focus? It is made up of five key facets. 'L' is for lead generation; really step one in the sales process. 'A' stands for appointment setting and booking in business to ensure consistency of results. 'S' is that magical sales process itself - ensure that you have it streamlined for efficiency and maximum return. 'E' is that intangible enthusiasm or energy that you bring to the sale. Bring energy in the right fashion and the ledger will be looking very solid and in the green. Lastly, the close off part of this process is the 'R', the referral. Asking for future business to ensure that you continue to perform can easily turn one sale into many with the right referral ask in place. This together makes up the 'LASER' Focus, set your laser beam on success and don't stop until you get there. Now beam me up Scotty!

In the world of sales the words control and concern need to be at the epicentre of all of your actions, especially when it comes down to a team's performance. Too often in the KPI driven arena, people can cling onto items which are out of their control or that should not even concern them. It is an escape route for them, an easy way to face failure as they can blame it on something else. I never accept this way of thinking, I will also challenge the control and concern 'cop-out' with the control and concern Venn diagram; see page 69. What you need to do in sales is first establish what it is that is relevant to you, what is it that you should be concerned with - once you know what that is, then you establish what your controllable items are and you simply control them in relation to what concerns you. Sounds easy I know, but you will often see the opposite happen in reality. People will cling onto what they have no control over as their reasoning for failure. The number of times I have seen sales staff blame the weather for their poor result is borderline cringe worthy. So how do we combat this sales problem, we focus on the mid-point, the sweet spot, where control and concern meet in a synergistic mesh which screams success. We focus on areas we need to be worried about, i.e. the concern section and the areas where we can have a direct impact, the controllable. If we do this well, the sales machine will roll on.

Challenge

Put simply; contact double the number of people that you contacted yesterday. If you contacted zero yesterday - contact one today. To double your contacts, double your work rate. Be more clever about where you spend and where you waste your time. You will quickly see where you are spending and wasting time after you have viewed your day with a critical set of eyes.

Control/Concern Venn diagram

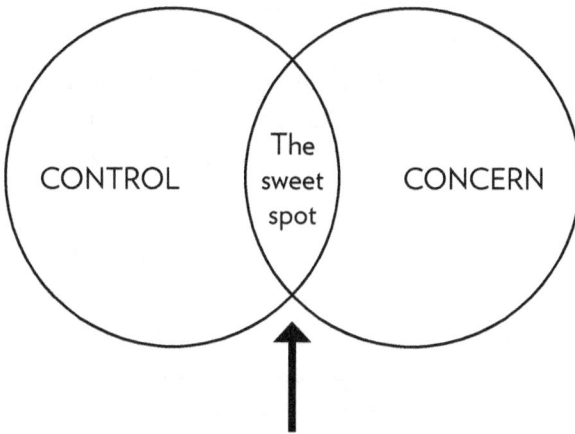

CONTROL   The sweet spot   CONCERN

By focusing on the midpoint you ensure all focus on what all can control, e.g. the amount of phone calls all make and what does concern all e.g. upselling products to your current clients.

Appointments are gold

To ensure that you are setting yourself up for success, you need to walk into businesses and not sit in yours waiting and hoping. Waiting might get you some sales, but booking up appointments a day or two prior to making them will definitely bring success.

It is easy to book an appointment - you just need to find a lead and then get into some needs analysis over the phone before inviting them in to meet you or your business. It may be you visiting them or the other way around. Essentially, you are asking them, *"can I have the opportunity to sell you my product or service?"* Never forget that you are also giving them the potential opportunity to change their lives, their business or their mind-sets.

After your lead generation you need to ensure that you can work the phones effectively. Research and create a sales script of how you should respond to questions. Teach this method to your staff, your team or even use it as a refresher for yourself. I have directly managed health clubs where I ensured that we would walk into at least thirty appointments in a day. Imagine how easy it would be to sell one membership when you have thirty appointments to sell to.

You trainers out there, ensure that you walk into consults, health screenings etc. daily. Managers, ensure you are walking into corporate business meetings daily to try to increase your reach and presence. Sales people walk into hot appointments every day and you will see your sales' numbers sky rocket.

When you make sure that there is enough time in your day to appointment set, you are making sure your sales continue to flow. Setting up what is called an appointment drive is the best way to see results in this category. An appointment drive (or A-Drive for short) is a time where you are solely focused on calling people and booking them in for appointments or chats/catch ups. Once again, we use the term catch-up or chat, because it has connotations of a friendly greeting/interaction. That is what you want to make the prospect feel, so remember you talk *catch-up* and *chat* on the phone even though it is an appointment drive. The word appointment reminds people of the dentist and that can be a scary thought (I know it certainly is for me, in stage two of my root canal...)!

It is always of key importance to ensure that prior to any A-Drive you organise what I like to call an L-Drive, a time where your sole focus is on lead generation and you have no distractions whatsoever. L-Drives must be as methodical as A-Drives, with times locked in and a tangible numbers of leads to be recorded in that timeframe.

The old saying 'fail to prepare, prepare to fail' rings true when we talk about this part of the business. So what do I need to do? Ask yourself how many appointments do you need to be able to do enough business per day?

Firstly, you need to understand the three key ratios that come into play when you talk appointments.

1. Contact to appointment or CA ratio: How many people you need to contact versus how many appointments you get.

2. Show ratio: from the ones that you speak to, who say they will come in and see you, how many actually show up

3. Close ratio: of those that *do* show up, it is how many you end up actually selling to.

Now, how many appointments do you need to get the sales you desire?

Be careful, it's not as easy as five appointments equal five sales. Some appointments don't show up (Show Ratio) and some do show up but you don't sell to them (Close ratio). So with that in mind, think again: how many appointments do you need per day for your business to be a success?

Some guidelines for ratios are:

- C: A RATIO – GOOD 40% GREAT 50%+

- SHOW RATIO: GOOD 65%, GREAT 75%

- CLOSE RATIO: GOOD 70%, GREAT 80%+

So now, if your goal is two sales per day and you take your ratios into consideration, work your way backwards and then you can see why you sometimes need to overcompensate on the appointments' side of things. An understanding of the ratios is crucial from a training and development viewpoint, because with the right know-how you can tweak your training requirements, based on what the ratio analysis says. To understand your business, you must understand the ratios.

Challenge

Establish your goal number of sales for a day – then decide the appointment goal that will be necessary to arrive at the desired goal.

If your goal for monthly sales is four and you adhere to the *'good'* ratio percentages on the previous page, how many appointments would you need per day?

Here's an example: As the new business owner of a sales-training business, I need four sales per month to keep me afloat in my initial year. Going on the good percentages in the guidelines I would need the following:

(Working backwards) Four sales monthly divided by 0.7 divided by 0.65 is 8.7.

So I need nearly nine appointments per month to get four sales. It adds up quick!

Don't forget that what you require sales-wise on a monthly or yearly basis relates to you and your business directly, so you must decide on what that magic number is.

Just ask

Growing up as a kid, I often heard the saying "presumption is the mother of all f*ck ups"; yes Irish households have a lot of swearing! But this is not the case in sales, in fact it is just the opposite; sometimes you need to presume. You need to presume this person is interested until told otherwise. There is no point in creating problems before you actually have any. So, that's why you want to presume that everyone is ready to buy and for those that are not you can merely seem shocked when they say they don't want to buy. Because you are selling to yourself as well as to them, you should actually be surprised when someone doesn't want your amazing product.

Don't ever be afraid to ask for a sale. While I was in membership sales, I can't count the number of times someone walked in and said *"now I'm not here to join today"* and by the end of our conversation they leave with a backpack, a smile and a contract – it's crazy. They are really just saying things like this as a defence-mechanism, it's their sales tool for themselves and they use it as an insurance policy to advertise the fact that they are in charge and they are the ones making the decisions. That is totally fine, but as I said, it doesn't mean they can't join today.

Just ask. Ask why? Ask how? Ask and ask and ask again. Dig deep and keep digging deeper, for the real reason that they can't commit today. A lot of times people will say they cannot commit because they have been conditioned to say that; to avoid change, but you are here to provide change. Ask for every sale, every day. Don't be shy; don't be scared that it will cause you to lose business. Let me give you a real hint about what will lose you plenty of business quicker than asking for a sale too many times and that's not asking for any sales!

I have seen great rapport builders become terrible sales people after they have talked themselves out of every sale because they could not *ask for the sale*. It is not hard to do - all you need to do is finish your pitch with a call to action like *'OK, let's get this started'* and then get their approval and move on. When you get to closing, ask and then quickly shut up. Don't talk too much or you could talk yourself out of the sale and you don't want that, now do you.

Challenge

This challenge is simple: ask one person to do business with you or ask one person to buy something from you. Just ask, then shut up.

Scripting

There are only two outcomes for any call:
you sell them on your why or they
sell you on their why not.

Scripted listening

The phone can be your best friend or your worst enemy. If you are new to sales or working with sales phone calls, my biggest piece of advice is to make some really bad calls today, right now before it's too late. Get them out of the way and under your belt and from there on in it can only get better. What I have seen happen in the past is people put off calling because of the excuse of wanting to know everything and know exactly what to say first. Scrap that - pick up the phone and start making mistakes and learning as you go. Here's my top tip number two, before you get into the scripting, just treat everyone on the phone like a friend of yours and your calls will flow more smoothly. You are in control of the call's direction so don't panic.

To put you all at ease, my first two calls were *terrible*. The first phone call I made to a prospect really tested me; I had just arrived from Ireland and my Aussie twang was probably not up to scratch yet and when I spoke to my first prospect he had some stern words for me. Firstly, he responded to my *'hey mate, it's just Shane calling…'* with *'Shane, I am not your mate'…* The answer to this was definitely not in my script so I stumbled along until he eventually asked in a bemused way, *'Where are you calling from, like what country?'*, as if to say my accent was so strong I must be cold calling him from a call centre in Ireland. That was my first call. My second was to a prospect called Rebecca who it turned out was our receptionist, who had put her details down on a lead template and who took my call while she was on reception and I was in the call centre. She continued to play along and then opened the door in hysterics, laughing. Safe to say after these two calls I could have been dismayed but I simply said to myself, well they can only get better from here and they did!

You are calling with the purpose of selling them on your why. They may try to counteract your why with their why not but you must persist. This is especially true in the fitness industry, where we know our product is a must for all people. I will continue to push fitness as long as I can, because I have seen the positive results it brings to people's lives and to their families' lives.

Most companies will have a phone script for you to follow which helps your calls flow smoothly. However, and this is the caveat here, you must, without fail and every time, make the phone script your own. If the script has the word spectacular in it and you never say that word, change it for a synonym that you *do* use, or else it will sound forced. The same goes with the questioning process. One of the first questions most calls start with is, *'How are you going today?'* or similar and I have witnessed this go totally wrong when people are completely immersed in scripting. The prospect on the other end responded with *"not good actually, I have just lost out on my dream job due to lack of experience"* to which the sales consultant responded with *'Fantastic, so the reason for my call today is…'* As you can imagine it went pear-shaped pretty quickly and ended in the prospect hanging up and complaining afterwards. This was all because the sales consultant was reading from a script and doing so with extreme diligence but they weren't listening whatsoever. Remember, the script is there to guide you and to keep you on track so you ask the relevant questions, but it's not there for you to read from verbatim.

A fitness sales call should include the following five points, to ensure success and all the rest is you building rapport, listening and guiding the call. The following five questions will help you assess the quality of your lead. The five keys to fitness phone mastery are:

1. Location (do you live or work nearby, are you in the neighbourhood? Are we are convenient for you? Travel options etc.)

2. Exercise (what type, how often, where, past history and future goals. Really delve into this to maximise the next part. This should be a large portion of the call, if they give you permission)

3. Soft sell (If you enjoyed it here, could you see yourself as a member? Good to hear you are looking to get started, we can discuss this further when you pop down to see us)

4. Appointment (So which time would suit you best to come along; offer an alternative choice between one time and another, as you are pretty busy. Ensure you explain why they are coming down and what you are going to do for them in the meantime)

5. Referral (Ask *who* they *will* bring along with them, presumptive language ensures you double up your sales opportunities.)

If you can make sure that you touch on all of these points while on a fitness sales call, then you are on the right track to ensuring sales' success. The other thing you need to nail down here is your rapport building skills; listening techniques are crucial. For example, if you call and you hear a baby crying in the background, the fact that your fitness centre offers child-minding services could be a great entry point into the call, *'oh I can hear you have your hands full with your little one there; you'll be glad to hear we have a crèche on site and relaxation facilities too, so you can let the hair down'*. Other than those points, you need to make a lasting impression so that the prospect wants to meet you because you are nice, intriguing, friendly, interesting, well versed in your product and all the above. From here on you will win.

Challenge

Develop a quick sales script for your business that best represents what you do. Ensure it covers the five key steps to mastery, in at least some respect. It could vary depending on your product offering i.e. if you own a sales consultancy business in the fitness industry you may ask something under the 'R' section for referral. *'Ok Chris, it is great that you are coming down to chat about what we can do for your business. Let me ask you, who among your business' contacts or friend's network can you think of who would also like to experience the benefits of our services? I will get their name and contact number and then let them know what I can do for them too, which I am sure they will appreciate. If it works out with them, you will also receive our referral deal!'*

Create a solid five step phone script based on your business/ services and make your first few 'bad/scary' calls to get them out of the way.

Deflection-naire

In your call you need to be asking all the questions as if you had a questionnaire you needed to fill out. You ask the questions because you want to lead the call in a way that you see fit. You want to direct the conversational flow in your favour. You can do this by ending your conversation with a question, so as to ensure that the call does not stagnate. However, some may respond and try to take the call in the direction they want it to go in: You might say: *"so what type of training do you do?"* and the prospect comes back with a quick *"I am just chasing the price, mate"*. All you need to do, is to reply that you have noted their request and that you will get to that later on in the call. In this way you can deflect the flow of the call back to where you want it to go. When you do this well, the questions that they were looking to ask will be long forgotten by the time you end the call and you will have worked your magic. Remember, in each call you make you are the conductor and the conductor does not alter the route based on their passengers. If there is a bus stop coming up, the ones who want to get off will and the rest will stay the journey. You can ensure all your prospects stay on the line and only get off when you are ready to let that happen.

I used to find that the physical act of standing up whilst making a phone call helped me as I could see things from a different perspective and I often felt a power differential as most of those I called would be sitting down, at work or at home while I was standing. It was just a simple mental trick that seemed to work well for me. What can you do, to feel like you are in control of the call?

Learn the art of deflection-questioning so you can be a phone assassin. If you can make sure that you are guiding the direction of your prospect, you are doing it right. Eventually, it will become second nature and you will always start out with the end already in mind. If your aim is booking an appointment, then nothing will get in your way.

In a recent sales training session that I facilitated for some new sales staff, they mentioned that they couldn't get leads over the phone because people weren't interested. My response was that when people say they are not interested now, it doesn't mean that they won't be interested next week, next month etc. So to test this, we called local businesses to see if we could get our foot in the door and get a personal lead from the receptionist, who answered the call, to try to sell them a gym membership. The first one answered and said she wasn't interested however I led the call and continued asking repeatedly for her number by saying *'so what was your mobile number 04..., 04...?'* She finally caved in and gave me her details. It just goes to show that if you can get the details of someone who is not interested now; imagine how easy it will be when they are interested. Stay in the fight and don't ever give up. Not interested now, does not mean not interested ever.

Challenge

Next time you face a tough call or a tough prospect - stay in the fight and do not give up until you get your desired result. You'll see how easy it is. Maybe it'll be when you're applying for a job: *"sorry all the positions are filled"* - *"ok what other positions do you have available that I can put my hand up for? In fact, I can come by today and see you in person so you can see how interested I am face to face. When works for you?"* Push until you cannot push anymore.

We don't talk money

Money, money, money – money! You don't want to discuss this topic in detail over the phone with a prospect. That's because people who see cost as the deciding factor are thinking with their red brain and you want them to think about the emotional connotations towards the product and act from their green brain. You don't sell on promotion; you sell on *emotion*.

This is where you examine true cost versus true value. If someone simply calls you to ask the price, they are doing so because they don't know what else to ask. They don't know how to initiate the conversation without asking that type of question. As a skilled phone guru you need to respond with your deflection technique and to make the conversation go down the path which you have forged.

In the fitness business you will get a lot of calls that ask how much does it cost per week to be a member. If your price (being a value-based product) is twenty-five dollars a week the same prospect will then ring a low-cost operator who sells their membership at five dollars per week. The ill-informed prospect will decide with their head that the five dollar option is the best. However, you cannot make this decision without first seeing the locations, checking out the atmosphere or vibe and what is on offer. So in short, that is why you don't quote prices over the phone; it is way too vague and generic and it is also too available as a measuring tool for the ill-informed. You owe it to your prospects to invite them in and to open their eyes. You don't want them to make the wrong decision. Even if you *are* a low cost operator you are using price as a tool after the fact, but firstly you must build value based on emotion.

If you were buying a child's car seat would you search for the cheapest or the safest?

If you are buying food do you look at the nutritional content or just the price?

If you are getting health insurance do you get the cheapest one without dental, knowing that you will need dental work in the future?

We owe it to the prospect to invite them down and to give them all of the information so that they can make an informed decision. Why makes you buy, what gives you squat!

You must understand your value proposition and what exactly it is that separates you from the rest; is it that you provide a fully functional studio, with a childminding facility attached? It could be the fact that you have full length mirrors and hair-straighteners; for some that can be a huge value add. Try to isolate what it is that you have that may be a large value piece of the puzzle. To create value for the customer, you must show them what it is that you offer and, most importantly, how it can positively affect their lives. Focus on how it will help to develop that person and how it may contribute to their overall happiness or well-being. This is 'showing the value'. The value-add should become almost tangible, because you can sell it so well, you should almost be able to hold it. If you can see it in your mind, then you can hold it in your hand. That phrase is great but when it comes to value you must see it not only in your mind, but you must paint the picture in someone else's mind. A case in point to demonstrate this is when I was involved in the opening of a new health club, here in Western Australia. The site was selected, the build had begun and the hype was increasing. Pre-sales began and it kicked off with a bang: we sold an empty building, a construction site full of dust, a few CAD drawings and some marketing of what it would become, once complete. We sold the dream, what this club could become and what you could become along with us. In that particular pre-sale, the team and I managed to break two company records, to my knowledge. Firstly, the largest pre-sales memberships' volume - selling just over two and a half thousand memberships and secondly, and which I am not as proud of, was the longest delayed pre-sale lasting nearly six months. There was a stage where I felt as though I would be managing a building-site for eternity but thankfully we managed to open our doors and it was a roaring success. The value we created based on how someone could achieve their goals came down to making the future seem tangible today. Two thousand five hundred people not only saw it in their minds but they too felt it in their hands. You must create value in order to create customers.

Challenge

Ring around some local fitness providers to see how they respond. Ring local personal trainers and ask them purely for their price and see what different responses you receive. Based on these calls, see how you can separate yourself from the competition.

Objection Handling

I once knew a bouncer who called himself an ejection technician. Welcome to the world of excuse management.

Walk in the prospect's shoes

For many of those in the fitness industry, the scariest part is dealing with objections.

I find, however, that when you look at them as challenges instead, you can make them into a fun negotiation process. What is an objection? Well, it is defined as, 'an expression or feeling of disapproval or opposition, a reason for disagreeing.' This is what you need to get over and what you need to master. It is only an expression or 'feeling' of disapproval, so you can change this feeling by doing right by the prospect.

Sometimes you need to see things from someone else's point of view and not your own. There are times when you need to see what they want, what they think they want and try to join the two up or create a cross-section of the two. Some people will come to a fitness centre thinking they want to swim, but when you look at it closely and break it down, they may want to build their shoulder strength. They can definitely do this by swimming but they could also do various other activities to increase shoulder strength. If your facility doesn't have a pool, I'm pretty sure you would be interested in delving into the real why of their call and teasing out that detail to use in your objection handling.

We are in the excuse management business. I can still remember a bouncer back in my home town of Cork who referred to his job as an ejection technician, because he threw so many people out of clubs. I always tell new sales staff, in training, that you are excuse managers and that is it. All you have to do is ensure that you do not let people cave in to their excuses; you need to work around the excuses together, with them and show them that those excuses are surmountable.

Some people have real objections and concerns, but the overwhelming majority are just creating excuses for themselves that are not based in reality. Instead their excuses are based on their own negative self-talk. What if I don't use it, what if I don't train every week, what if I move house, what if I lose my job and can't afford it any more. You name it, I've heard it. What these people don't seem to ask themselves is, what if I don't start today where will I be in two years' time? Some people will surprise you when it comes to the objection handling process. I think back to a time when I had a gentleman in his mid-20s in front of me who looked as though he already had a hard life behind him. When I asked him roughly how much he could afford a week, he said; *about 90 bucks a week*. I couldn't believe it because our prices were miles cheaper than that and I honestly didn't think he had that much money to spare. When I discussed his needs in depth he opened up to me and said that up until that week, he had been a self-confessed drug addict and had spent about ninety dollars a week on drugs. Now, he wanted to spend that on something positive rather than something negative and if he didn't have it to spare, he also wouldn't be tempted to spend it on old bad habits. Great guy and a great idea! That same month we were doing a promotion with a local charity where you could donate ten bucks to the charity to receive a free month's membership. I was at the point where I was fed-up of dealing with people who would haggle over the ten-dollar donation and this gentleman gave me fifty dollars towards the charity, just because. It was refreshing to see that some people don't make excuses for themselves. As he said, he had made them for himself long enough.

Think of what might be an issue for this prospect and try to pre-frame that issue with subtle cues and resolutions. It might be a personal training client who you may believe has issues with the price. Test the waters with a litmus test about what their current spend is. Once you know where they are 'wasting' money, you can show them how to save money by spending on you! Ironic isn't it.

Challenge

List at least eight of the most likely objections for your product or service and show the ways in which you would counteract this feeling of disapproval to buy. You might think eight is a lot at first, but as time goes by, you will see that you come across some ridiculous objections.

Objection   Solution

_____

_____

_____

_____

_____

_____

_____

You could just be a nice guy

Objections come in all shapes and sizes and some are altogether very strange. I have heard a mixed bunch and while it's safe to say most are what I consider the norm, a few stand out in my memory.

The first was the woman who mentioned that she couldn't join because she had to double check if it was OK with her dog, some people really do treat pets like they are a part of the family I suppose. There was another one which I can only break down, as the man who wanted me to be a 'nice guy' and give him a break. This particular individual wanted everything on his terms and for free, which I get. However, when you run a business, you run it to be successful and profitable. He wanted me to deal with him on his terms but I needed to use my deflection questioning to achieve success.

There's a story doing the rounds about a 'gentleman' (and I use the term loosely) who was a repeat offender. He would come into our fitness centre for free by using whatever method he could. He'd sneak in, use free passes (numerous types disregarding the one-use only T's & C's associated with said pass), come with a mate who could charm our receptionist or any other way he could; the one way he never seemed to try was actually paying casually or joining. Now, I have a general rule of thumb: if someone comes into my business and expects something for free and then they are demanding, they generally end up paying full whack whatever alternatives might be available. If someone comes in with the right approach and is willing to pay to access the facilities, I would initially let them in for free as a reward to them.

On this chap's seventh scammed entrance I stopped him and asked him to grab a seat. I presented the options he had to him:

pay casually, join or go elsewhere (in the nicest possible way). He was not impressed with my options and said couldn't I just *be a nice guy* to which I responded with the biggest smile I could and the nicest attitude, *'OK, just twenty dollars, mate'*. He continued to argue and disagree until I asked him one simple question: what do you do for a job? He responded, he was a mechanic. This was music to my ears as I wanted to get my car serviced at the time. German cars and the servicing fees are crazy and all that! So, when I asked him if he could service my car for free and be a nice guy, he understood and paid. Sometimes you can be nice but you have to remember, you are in business. Don't be taken advantage of, you deserve better than that.

Challenge

In the spirit of this section, try being as nice as you can today. Who knows, the world may reward your new 'nice' approach to the day? Being outwardly nice helps people to see you as approachable and you may even receive more interest from clients or future clients who may open up to you.

Pre-Empt the issues

To me this is one of the main changes you can put in place today to help increase your closing skills. Objections and problems will always be there and that you can't change them, but what you can change is *when* you talk about them. My advice is to deal with them way before you get to the sales pitch and the scary stuff, because that is when people are going to use objections to counteract you. If you start to pre-empt problems subtly in your needs analysis or chat or wherever you can outside of the sales process, you should have much more success. A good example of this is when you find out that a female personal training client may come from a culture where men have a domineering approach to financial decisions. Thus if you are trying to sell your PT services, they may give you the objection of having to speak to their hubby first. They have a case of COWS (Cannot operate without spouse). This can be a crippling objection, if you let it be.

How do you counteract these issues? The answer is to deal with it early. PT and potential client sit down to have a chat. You notice that the lady has a nice wedding ring on and mention how great the ring looks. From there you can ask the question about her husband and if he knows that she is here chatting with you. You find out if he is supportive and once you have those two answers sitting right you can begin to play on them. You can refer to her 'super supportive husband' and keep dropping this hint prior to your sales pitch. Now when she tries to object to the sale at point of sale because she needs to speak to her husband, you can remind her that her super supportive husband is great and would not have an issue with her being happy! Also, just get her to give him a call while she is sitting there. Don't be scared to ask and don't be scared to sit and wait.

A sale is like a phone number and if you get any one digit wrong you will never connect. All of these pieces are digits, so you must ensure that you get every digit right. The objection handling piece is one of the numbers towards the tail end of the process but it is a crucial piece.

The process of pre-empting objections can be a lifesaver as it helps grind down the objections with extreme subtlety. When it comes to getting the deal done, price can be another problem area. What about if you could discuss price, in a non-challenging way before getting into your price presentation? It could come about organically by the use of a few simple questions such as, do you think you can afford fifteen bucks a week? If the prospect answers yes, then they can't really say it is unaffordable later on because they have agreed that this could work. If you follow this sort of questioning during a sales negotiation when you are trying to close at the end, well, the prospect might see the prices you present and simply say that they are out of their budget. At this stage you cannot back-track and ask a pre-emptive question. So make sure you ask early!

Sales pitches are like a game of chess; one person makes a move then the next. Get comfortable taking your time in this process and deciphering what each move means and how to respond. Don't jump in too quickly or make a move which you cannot recover from.

If they stump you with a strong objection, well then that is checkmate, if you get them to realise their objections are negligible then you have taken their king.

Challenge

Before your next next consultation, meeting or similar, look at all the potential pitfalls and see how you could deal with them before they rear their ugly heads.

Mindset

The world is the way you see it;
if you see it with clouds it will rain,
however if you chose to see the sun,
you will get a tan.

If you see clouds - it will rain

The mind is an extremely powerful tool and in an industry such as fitness, where you are so often tested physically, you will also be tested mentally and you need to be prepared for that.

The fitness industry is based primarily around image and perception and these two factors can weigh heavy on people's minds. The trick is to ensure that your mind-set is a positive and beneficial one when it comes to training (gym) and work alike. Think of it this way: if you believed that you couldn't gain muscle and couldn't get stronger, well, that would become a part of your decision making process. It would mean that you probably wouldn't push as hard on those last one or two reps and you'd stop early; maybe you'd skip a few days because you believed it wouldn't really matter anyway. All of this has come solely from your belief that you cannot progress. The same is true in the working environment. If you think you can't hit a certain KPI or you think that it's unachievable, then it's a good bet that it will be. If you think that you cannot grow your PT business to over fifty sessions a week, once again, you won't. Because you don't believe in it, you won't try for it. You won't push when it gets hard; you won't grind day after day towards slowly achieving a goal. But do you know what? That grind and that daily grit is precisely what is required both in business and in fitness. We've all been there; a plateau where you feel as though you are stuck, stagnant and beginning to get 'too comfortable'. Well, simply get unstuck and get uncomfortable. It's all in the wording: we say we are too comfortable as if it's a bad thing but yet when we say uncomfortable, we also see it as negative. Clearly it is not, it's the opposite of 'too comfortable'. Get uncomfortable and you will grow.

What does getting uncomfortable mean for you? Putting yourself out there more, to try to attract new business? Speaking on stage at networking/business events even though you hate public speaking (that was me!), or simply sacrificing an hour on Sunday to plan your work week? Whatever it is, find it and do it.

Terminology and self-talk are a part of this. If you surround yourself with negative thoughts, people and ways you will become that, negative. Choose to be surrounded by people like you who want to win. The desire to win is something I discuss often, about having a real sense of being a winner. It's a predetermined notion that is based on your input and only you contribute to your win. I chose to win daily and you should too. Think about this example: I often hear people say they are drowning in their workload and that it is overwhelming. Instead of this you could say *I am excited by the opportunity to do more and I am facing so many new issues which I have not dealt with previously that this is a great learning opportunity*. In the same way you tweak that sentence, you can choose how you internalise the information. Self-talk is crucial; believe you are a winner, say it to yourself and be proud of it.

If you can adjust your way of seeing things, then you can adjust the way it is. I am a big believer in the world being the way you see it and if you see it full of clouds, then guess what, you'll get wet and it will hail and rain daily. However, you can decide to see the world full of sunshine and if you do, you will get a tan! See the sun and you will receive all its benefits. Let the sun shine down on you and step out from under the cloud of discontent. Just choose; choose to see sunshine. I take my sunglasses with me everywhere because I am ever the optimist!

Challenge

I once knew a manager from a different industry who would walk into the building and within minutes of his arrival people would know what the day's vibe would be, crap! If that manager was having a bad day, well, so was everyone else. This is just not fair; leave your negative vibes where they belong, somewhere else. Bring your best vibe!

Thinking about this has prompted me to review my behaviour and actions and I insist on checking in with myself daily.

Check your vibe! This is a saying I have put up in my office, right above the door. Without fail, every time before I leave the room to face an issue, be it to help a client or just to get a coffee, I check my vibe. Looking at those handwritten words remind me of how others can influence the feelings in a room and so I check in with myself to see how I'm feeling. If I am down and feeling sorry for myself, I make sure that when I leave that room, my team are uplifted by my vibe and not dragged down by my negative feelings. Check your vibe. Write it down somewhere that will help you remember, before you get into any situations where your vibe may be required. Check in with yourself daily and ensure your vibe is good.

The drive to work

Following on from the last section, where we talked about how the world is the way you view it; you can make this apparent in your approach to daily tasks and activities. I think back to two members of a senior leadership team as a striking example. When they were both given the same news, they took it very differently. Both were told they would be moving location and that their drive to work would be extended slightly. One of them, who I believe sees the world with sunshine, said *"Brilliant that gives me more time to listen to new motivation speeches, TED talks and even learn a new language on the way to work"*. The other said *"This is a disgrace, I hate traffic, I hate driving; this is unfair"*. Now, which of these two approaches and responses do you think will get you more results?

I use that example expressly to present this content to you in a user-friendly manner. It is not hard to switch your mind-set to a winning one; all it takes is conviction and a belief in the fact that you are going to improve. One of the leaders took this information and made it work for him, while the other held onto his historically developed inertia towards change and went the other direction.

If an outcome is preordained, why get upset about it. Why not accept it with open arms and see if it can become an advantage and not a hindrance.

As a Regional Business Manager, I get a vast amount of my phone calls dealt with whilst driving (hands free kit of course – stay safe!). I use this as a chance to connect with people over the phone when I can't look at emails or be distracted from anything except the road in front of me. I use this time to become efficient and effective. Sometimes I listen to some relaxation music; some motivational speeches or I practice a speech that I have to present. It is really all about the way you view it. I find that we all have many times in our day where we can be using our time more wisely. Whilst doing passive activities and actions I now add in another; so for example driving and using the hands-free kit to connect, walking on a treadmill and reading, having a shower and mentally preparing the day, just to name a few. All of this can be done in a safe and effective manner. We only have so much time in our day and you need to ensure that you can be a time master. Master time and you will master your day and yourself.

When my days were becoming hectic and I was struggling to master my time, I simply found another option, which was that if I left early enough in the morning so I would avoid the bulk of the traffic. So some mornings I just wake up earlier, get on the road earlier and arrive at my location (which thankfully has a gym, as it is a gym!) earlier. I can get a gym session completed, work on my writing, read a little, respond to some emails and be set up for my day all by 7.30 a.m. This is accomplished just by realising what I can do and not focusing on what I can't do. It can work in exactly the same way for you.

Forget all the reasons why it won't work and believe the one reason why it will!

Challenge

For the next week, wake up early and get on the road before the traffic. Get to your work location early. Do a gym session or work on you, all before 8 a.m.! If this isn't an option, make your drive time in the traffic a pleasant experience. Plan a TED talk you would like to listen to and have it ready for the car. If you need some down time in your day, turn everything off, sit in your car and work on breathing exercise whilst in traffic. Four seconds in, deep breaths, four seconds out exhale. Watch as the world becomes still and you along with it.

Preparing for the week

What do successful people do right? They prepare. I have spoken with so many successful fitness industry minds and usually, they all share one common denominator. At some time, usually on a Sunday, they prepare for the week ahead. For me this is based around organising my weekly critical path. Every week I make sure that I have a detailed plan about what I need to do, what outcomes I want to achieve and where I will be. This helps me from a scheduling perspective so I don't double-book myself and I can be sure I can visualise the week ahead and how it will unfold. I try my best to stick to this plan, but of course, sometimes a new 'fire' can crop up which means I need to reshuffle. This type of thing could be an urgent people issue, a staff shortage, an important new meeting with a business opportunity etc. The list is endless but I do try, above all else, to stick to my plan.

Sunday is a fun day so be sure you spend that time with your loved ones, doing what you love. For me it's about spending time with my partner, walking the dog, getting to the gym and having a nice lunch or brekky. Enjoy the time you have together. The mantra is: give 100% at work and then go home and give 100% to those you love. However, set aside one hour every Sunday that you will use to plan the upcoming week. You will quickly see what is required and what you will need to do to get the job done.

Personally, I like to focus on three 'big rocks', that is three main focus points that I must complete in my week and then three smaller 'rocks' which are still important but which can wait until the big rocks are dealt with.

It's worth noting that the small rocks cannot be moved until you get the big ones out of the way. This helps you to stop procrastinating. Normally, I put the scary, uncomfortable and difficult jobs as my big rocks because it ensures that I have to complete them early. I like to do difficult, challenging work first thing on a Monday morning and to not let it simmer until later. Trust me; you will just end up thinking about it all night, every night until you face it. Do it early and be done with it.

Challenge

Plan your week using the critical path of your working week. Where will you be, what will you do and how will you do it? What support, if any, will you require. Plan your three big rocks and three little rocks for the week and be honest to them.

This planner will serve as a quick reminder that will aid in your reflection and pre-planning. It's a great tool for all sales people, business people and fitness people. When you are ready in advance, this sets the tone for the week. When you are prepared, you are confident about what you need to do to accomplish your goals. How much better is this than coming in on a Monday morning, scattered and chasing after the week.

Referrals

*'Guest on arrival,
friend on departure'*

Guest on arrival, friend on departure

In the fitness business you *are* the service you provide. Essentially, you are in the service industry. I liken it to a hairdresser or barber. If you go to the barbers and your barber is in a bad mood, you can get a bad haircut, the same is true for a PT. Try to avoid this personalisation of your mood at work and keep it separate. You must abide by the mantra of 'guest on arrival, friend on departure'.

As far as I am concerned, this is one way in which you can really ensure success. People do business with people and you need to be a nice person, who others want to be around. People want to be around their friends (most friends at least). In short you need to enter into a type of friendship (professional of course) with your customers, clients and others. To do this you must simply be yourself; be open and be honest.

As a membership consultant, I have had people come back and invite me to events, birthdays and weddings on numerous occasions. Although I generally decline in order to try to keep the barriers of professionalism up, I have clearly created friend-ships. After that however, people began to see me as more than a salesperson and as a friend. This is what you want to achieve. When someone comes to your door, you may not know them from Adam but when they leave they *will* know you, and you them. I can walk back into many of the facilities where I have worked previously and strike up a friendly conversation with many of the people that I met years back.

Once all of the staff in your fitness club share this attitude, you can only succeed. Instill the importance of this in all of your staff, at a staff meeting. Show them the value of creating valuable work friendships. Keep the barriers up, yes, but showing the client or customer your honesty and vulnerabilities is not a bad thing.

If you can create a sense of friendship during the rapport building process, you are a sales pro. You know what it takes and you have the right approach. If I like you, more than the guy across the road, I would take out a gym membership with you because of that, even if the other club was cheaper. I know this because I do business with people. I'll give you the example of two coffee shops that were near a gym I once managed. There were two coffee shops, both with similar coffee and both right next door to one another, no real difference besides the price. Coffee shop A was about thirty cents more expensive, yet I went there every time because the people in there treated me better. They knew my name, they learnt my order and they would talk to *me*. I had no problem paying them an extra thirty cents because I was a guest on arrival and I became a friend on departure. Remember to personalise your service and to ensure that your staff are personable.

From a referral perspective, once you establish this solid relationship, the benefits will come in abundance. From now on these 'friends' are going to become your business builders, as they preach about you and make sure that you and your business are more and more recognised.

The best referrals you can get from a client are their friends and family members, so if you can make your clients feel like friends and family members of your business, you are already a step ahead of the rest.

Challenge

Create more than a sale; create a business friendship with the next prospect that walks into your business.

You don't have to be a family business to make people feel like they are part of a family.

Put a sign on your forehead

For many people referrals are an afterthought. Sometimes you get so caught up in the sales process and the thrill and joy of the sale that you completely forget to build for future business.

You might be in a tough negotiation with a client (current or potential), where you put all of your energy into trying to close the deal, thus forgetting about future deals and future business. You must ensure that you remind yourself about the future at all times.

In sales offices I have managed in the past, I would put a sign on the sales peoples' desks, on a door or on their computer, everywhere: Even on their forehead if I had to! This was to remind them *to ask for referrals*. We'd noticed that when we were busy, we wouldn't always ask for future business; we would simply forget. So we added in these safeguards to our daily routine; these little reminders ensured that we asked one hundred percent of the time. It increased our point of sale referrals drastically and thus ensured that, yes we were successful today, but we would also be successful tomorrow.

Referral leads are your strongest leads and are probably the most cost effective way of generating new business. We seem to look everywhere else, except right in front of our noses for future business.

Challenge

Every single time you have a client/customer or new prospect in your business, ask for a referral. Just ask - every time. If you normally only ask once in your pitch, ask on numerous occasions. Write yourself an organic natural sounding script, where you touch on referrals at least three times. You could do this in a gym membership sales pitch where you ask initially, do they have a friend that trains here (ask number one). Then mention mid-point that training with a friend increases motivation (ask number two), and then finally ask number three comes at the end where you ask, *"who are you going to refer; who are you going to invite down"* (ask number three)? Ask for future business at least three times in your next presentation.

Give them an incentive

The last thing that you need to do in the referral process is the easiest thing. Ensure you make it worth their while. First of all, you need to follow steps one and two beforehand. Once you have created the friendship, then you can put a sign on your forehead. Then, and only then, you should create an incentive that will increase the likelihood of referral business.

Create a referral sheet for you and what you do. This could be a form, a document, an online tool, or any manner of media that lets you capture referral lead data. Ideally, it would be great to achieve three referrals per sale or per client. That needs to be the goal. Ask your client who is the first person that they think of who could use your services as well as them; that will be your hottest lead. Next, ask them who among their direct friends, family and colleagues might have an interest in your services. After that, the onus is on you to activate that interest further.

There are many creative strategies that you can use. One important way to ensure that it is desirable to refer your product offering is to make it beneficial for the person who gives you the referral. The benefit could come in the way of a cost savings for that person, or some added value or extra benefit for them.

What sort of incentives could you create in your business model that might become effective and positive referral tools? Think outside the box; think differently, think laterally not literally.

What is it that you can create to increase the refer-ability of what you do? If you are a PT, could you offer complimentary sessions in return for new business? Could you create a free recipe book for anyone who refers one new client? Another attractive offer might be a personalised fitness program, once the client completes a referral sheet.

Challenge

Create a product offering that ensures your business is referable. What could you create or use within your business which could act as a referral tool? For the next sale you complete, *ask* for at least three referrals.

Marketing

*'Marketing without data is like driving
with your eyes closed'*

You are your business

I live in the world of sales, which is all about the short game and direct selling. Marketing however is what you do to excel over the long term. Marketing creates a need and ensures the longevity of your business offerings. If you don't focus on both sales and marketing, well, put simply, you won't succeed. However, the two are not mutually exclusive; they must coincide and operate hand-in-hand.

It is easy for me to understand all of the jargon and terminology, as I have a marketing degree behind me. However, what I found out while I was studying for that marketing degree was that in order to be a successful marketer you first need to become a successful sales person. As I have mentioned before, first you must be able to *'sell yourself'*. Marketing is the effort which you make to ensure that you have people's attention. It operates on the premise that, you can make it so that the customer sells to themselves rather than you having to sell to them.

I often think back to a comment which was made by a senior lecturer at my old university about my attendance. He said *'to this day, I have yet to see someone do so well but attend so little'*. This was due to the fact that I had to support myself and I was trying to pay my way through university. I was working full time as a regional sales specialist for a local business where I probably learnt more than I ever could in a university. Those skills that I picked up along the way were reflected in my academic results and success. In marketing you must, connect with other people, use B2B strategies, network and much more – all of which I did every day while working.

When I was working for that company back in Ireland, people would see me as the business, as the brand evangelist. They associated me with the business and the business with me. I *was* the marketing. I am still the marketing only this time around it is a different product, a different industry and a different company. However, the concept remains the same: you must be the business. If it is your own business, you even have more of an incentive.

Try to think of marketing through using new strategies. Have you tried LinkedIn, have you thought about attending fitness events and getting involved as a sponsor? Have you considered organising a free community boot camp? All of these simple ideas are solid marketing approaches and can also very easily become sales tools down the track.

Firstly, to find out what area you may need to work on, you must find out what your assets are and what weaknesses you may have. You must ensure that before you go to market, you complete an in-depth SWOT analysis. This is an analysis of your business' strengths, weaknesses, opportunities and threats. You can use a SWOT analysis to decide which marketing strategies you are going to pursue and which you feel will add value to your business offering. It also shows you where you may need to increase the work rate to ensure success.

In order to be a marketing specialist, first you need to sell, then market, and then sell again.

You need to be confident in your product and you also need to be ready to constantly market your product no matter what, whatever the current economy and no matter the current state of affairs. You are your business and you are the marketing department. Be you online, be you in person, be you at all times. Make sure *you are always on!*

Challenge

Create a marketing plan for your business starting with a basic SWOT analysis to see what the situation is and where you need to do some work.

Fill in the SWOT analysis below, making reference to either you as a person or you as a business. You should be able to fill in at least two to three points in each section and then delve into them in depth. Make sure that you actually think about this before you start filling it out. Be sure that what you write down is a reflection of the reality and don't be afraid to 'call out' any weaknesses. It is also worth getting a second, unbiased opinion on your SWOT to see what that second party has to say. Once you have both completed the analysis, compare the two sections to see if there are any major differences or similarities. This is interesting and can be confronting but is invaluable.

Personal Analysis

Strengths _____

Weaknesses _____

Opportunities _____

Threats _____

Secondary Analysis

Strengths _____

Weaknesses _____

Opportunities _____

Threats _____

Brand evangelist

What is a brand evangelist?

Well, an evangelist is a person who seeks to convert others to the Christian faith, especially by public preaching. From now on, you are going to convert someone to your business model by preaching. That will make you a brand evangelist, someone who is willing to preach about you and your business and do so publicly.

The best way to be a brand evangelist is to be strong in your product offering. Back yourself so much that your customers or consumers do the selling for you. Think about the recent phenomenon that is Pokémon Go. You don't often see millions of dollars in advertising spend, but you do see Pokémon players posting publicity, basically advertising for the product, free of charge, because they believe in it.

How can you make your business go viral? How do you make your business sell itself? The answer is simple; make it worth someone's while. Make sure it exceeds all and every expectation that they have ever had. I recently became a brand evangelist for a pretty famous restaurant in Freemantle, Bib and Tucker (see I am evangelising it even now!). I got a side of potatoes which had garlic cloves; I don't often eat garlic cloves, so when I was finished there was essentially a side order of garlic cloves on the plate. The waitress took the dish but the manager spotted it. He came over and apologised for the excessive garlic; in fact he was apologising for a problem that, to be honest, I hadn't even noticed. They then offered me a free drink at the end of the meal and when I ordered it they also made sure that my partner got one on the house as well. What a nice gesture, fixing a problem before I could even have had the chance to complain about it. All too often, we wait for problems to occur before fixing them.

Why not get ahead of the curve and avoid reacting in crisis mode. Now I recommend anyone to go to the restaurant and to try their dishes; the pumpkin gnocchi main course is delish!

Problems and complaints can become an opportunity for you to evangelise customers. Don't be afraid to deal with these moments head on.

In order to achieve success in this modern society you must stand out from the rest or else fail - disappearing into obscurity. To do so, you must excel, you must be different and you must be strong in what you do. If you can create brand *apostles* in different countries, different regions and different demographics, your likelihood of success will increase tenfold.

Think of whom you can look to when you are thinking about creating your team of apostles. Who are the thought leaders, decision makers and early adopters in your field and how can you speak to them? Preach brothers and sisters, preach!

Challenge

Think about who you could evangelise in your field. Who can you target so they get on board and speak on behalf of your business? Who can help sell your product offering organically? Think of twelve people who could work with you today. Who will be your twelve brand apostles?

Local Area Marketing (LAM)

To be sure your marketing campaign is a success, you need to ensure it is aimed at the right demographic, i.e. that it is tailored for your market and your locale.

Local Area Marketing (LAM) is a great way to ensure that you canvas the exact areas and demographics that you are aiming to target.

Make sure that your message is tailored precisely to the person you are trying to reach. If you offer group fitness classes and Cross Fit at your facility, you would probably advertise both products but to different groups. Search criteria can be a great tool in this process. As an example, on Instagram you could search for related terms and then actively target these people. You can include terminology on Facebook with paid adverts which lets you enter the search criteria you want, based on sex, age, interest etc. Paper-based advertising and flyer drops can also be tailored to a particular area and this can guarantee that the results are in your catchment area (the area in which you feel like your demographic is based). Depending on your product, the general catchment area could be up to fifty kilometers. However, if your product offering is specialised the catchment area might be much broader and in that case adding an on-line element obviously helps to break these geographical barriers – it's all based in the cloud.

A targeted campaign can yield much higher results than a generic campaign which is not tailored towards any one particular group. Remember, you cannot be everything to everyone but you must be something to someone. Tailor your approach specifically towards one group and then work diligently on that group. After that, change your offering and target a new group and repeat this until you achieve mass success.

What does your local area marketing plan currently look like? Have you actually established your catchment area? Lastly, do you know exactly who you want to speak to, what you want to say and how you want to say it?

During this process you need to decide on your specific *"voice"*. You should decide exactly what you want to say to which groups. You need to be able to talk in detail to that segment. Segmenting your market into different groups can also make your life so much easier. As an example, a personal trainer may offer four basic products – personal training, boot camp, ladies only classes and online coaching. Each of these has a different marketing context and tone. More importantly they all need to be delivered in a different fashion. The PT can be generic to an extent, obviously the ladies' classes are tailored towards a specific segment of the population and the marketing would reflect this in its voice, tone, colouring and imagery etc. Keep all of this in mind as you build your LAM.

Challenge

Design your business LAM. Define your voice.

What do you have to say? Who will you say it to?

Business Acumen

I'm not a businessman;
I'm a business, man.

Jay Z

Understand you operate in the business world

The great thing about being in the fitness industry is that you get to wear sports' clothes. This is a common misconception held by many but it doesn't mean that you cannot do well while wearing sports' gear. But be careful, I must draw your attention to the fact that you are primarily in business and then in fitness.

A great salesperson could easily become a PT and give it a fair crack, even if their skill-set as a trainer was non-existent to start with, but a poor salesman who knows everything about hypertrophy and body sculpting, until the cows come home, is no use if they can't build rapport, talk and sell. In this state they are not valuable to the business.

Being in fitness is being in business. You wear two hats: that of the business person and that of the fitness representative. So that you are sure that you know what you are doing, I suggest that you get some sort of business training first, some sort of basic business knowledge. I would recommend getting involved in a basic business course that will suffice as a pre-requisite. It is crucial to be familiar with business terminology, with the concepts of business, as well as the laws of business. You could take a night course if needs must, alongside your full time work, but don't skip this step. It is going to help you maximise your outcomes. It may cost you a few thousand dollars but it will guarantee that you increase your earning potential exponentially. Online courses are also readily available these days where you can enrol and learn as you work.

Everything from ripping apart a profit and loss account with scrutiny, to dealing with a serious performance management issue needs to be well within your reach if you want to be able to conduct your business at peak performance. You must sharpen up your tools of the business trade prior to embarking and whilst embarking upon any fitness venture.

If you are not earning you should be learning. Always aim to increase your knowledge base, increase your skill-set and thus increase your potential. If you currently have a basic business course certificate, get a degree. If you already have a degree, then get an MBA. If you aim to keep learning and keep upgrading your mental software, you will remain current. If you don't you will become obsolete a bit like computer software. You must update software to stay current and the same is true for the human psyche. You don't want to be a Nokia 3210 forever.

Challenge

Understand the basic business terminology below – just Google the terms if you get stuck!

Return on investment(ROI)	Net performer score (NPS)
EBITDA	Cost per lead (CPL)
Pay per click (PPC)	Secondary Revenue Source
Attrition rate	Marketing Mix
SWOT Analysis	Social media strategy
The 4 P's of Marketing	Sales funnel (pipeline)
Financial year	Closing ratio
Show ratio	Catchment Area

Track and monitor quarterly

If you don't understand what a financial year or a quarter is, you will need to brush up on your business acumen. You need to be astute in this area, because this is where you can be more frugal on the expenses side of the business and this in turn helps to reduce operating expenditure. You can also aim to add additional revenue sources to your product mix. For example, a personal trainer who up until now has only offered one-on-one sessions could aim to add an additional revenue stream. It could come from boot camp sessions, online clients, meal plans, competition preparation, mind-set training, coaching of new trainers or in fact anything. There are many varied avenues you can look at for pursuing new business ventures and for remoulding your current business.

You should aim to increase your revenues each and every quarter, and to have at least one new product offering come out in each quarter. So, Quarter one may have a heavy online element, with a sales focus on social media. Quarter two could see the launch of your boot camp series. Quarter three should have another element to it; maybe it could be focused on bringing in revenue from education such as giving seminars to new trainers or something similar. Lastly in Quarter four, you could add some sort of client meet up or awards dinner as a revenue source and retention tool. This is just a quick snapshot of some of the things you could do. You could even launch a book as part of your major quarterly actions.

Understanding the importance of this will ensure that you not only run a business, but you run a profitable business and just as importantly, you can track trends and prepare for any future change based on said trends. Is it useful to track last year's performance, for example, versus this current year's performance; has anything changed drastically that could have caused a change in performance? Without this know-how and backstory, you cannot predict future trends or movements.

Challenge

Plan your business quarterly. Estimate spending and earnings for each quarter and compare and contrast them to the same quarter from last year. Aim to see growth in the earnings' figures. The aim is to establish year on year growth. If your growth is stagnating, investigate bringing in new revenue streams. What extra revenue streams could you incorporate into your business or personal earnings?

The key parameter is growth.

Seek guidance, seek more

Look around you. Who is doing what you do, but better? Who do you look up to? What is it that they are doing that is slightly different from you? My advice is to emulate the success of others. There is no shame in trying to learn from others and in seeking guidance. Just ask. Once again, you would be surprised how many people will want to help. Whatever level you are on, call and ask that person who is succeeding, if they could share a best practice. Are they doing what you do, but with a minor tweak that is yielding a major result. That is what you want to know.

This falls under the heading of **do more, be more, see more.** You have to constantly seek to improve upon the past year, the past month and the past day, in order to experience any sort of growth. I have always looked for leaders within the world in which I operate. If I am looking to develop a mobile application for example, then I seek out a successful mobile application developer. It's that easy! This is what I have done in the past, as well as in a recent project in which I was involved; watch this space. I had an idea based around mobile applications, so I asked around to see who has already developed a mobile app in a similar space. I got in touch with this person and we discussed our different points of view and shared information. I had no hesitation in doing this and the other person was more than open to chatting to a like-minded person. It is not scary to ask. Get involved and seek guidance. I was open from the get go to the fact that my product might be in a similar space as theirs and they were fine with sharing their wisdom.

Asking will take you a long way in life. One thing is certain, if you don't ask you won't get. What is it you want to eventually work towards completing? Often in this industry, the new staff who are coming on board have a five-year plan that involves their opening of some sort of fitness facility. I don't mention the fact that they have no business skills whatsoever, cannot read a profit and loss statement and don't know what an investor is, but what really gets me is that they refuse to ask for help. I have only ever met one person who wrote in their five-year plan that they hoped to be halfway towards opening their own facility and to be learning from people who have already opened facilities.

If I think back over the last year, at least five new employees said they would like to open a facility off their own backs, yet not one of them asked for any feedback on the process up until now, or even enquired about what I have learned from opening a health club with over two and a half thousand pre-sales members. The funny thing is, I would have happily shared some of the tools that I have used to ensure such a successful pre-sale, some of the pre-open pit falls and other bits of knowledge which I think would be beneficial, but again, if you don't ask you don't get. If you want to do something, ask someone who has already done it.

Challenge

Find someone local who has done what you want to do and ask them if they can sit down for a coffee to have a chat and if they could share what has worked for them. Always look for someone who is successful and whom you would like to emulate. If you can't find a local option, scour the internet until you find someone and connect with them online.

Teams

People are the lifeblood
of an organisation

The Right people

It's all about the people but believe me; some people will really push you! Having said that, people are the real reason you will either achieve success or stagnate in your business. Worse still you may not even get off the ground with your venture if you base it on the wrong people.

So, if we all agree that the people part of this piece is of utmost importance, do we always pick the best people? No. Sometimes, we end up making quick decisions and end up giving positions to people with no experience, no ambition and no 'will set'.

This is a 'passionate' industry but, surprisingly, you will meet a lot of people in it who have no passion. How on earth are you going to inspire someone to change their fitness habits when you clearly haven't changed yours? How will you motivate someone to lose weight, by training four times a week, when you do not practice what you preach?

The people you choose must, and always must, believe in the product and what it can do for their clients. This needs to be the starting point of any hiring process. You must also communicate that the position may not just be this one position, but it could be a catalyst for people to progress further. What is that person's 'why'? Sales people who don't make sales are simply data entry administration staff and personal trainers who don't train themselves are no better than a demonstrational guide on paper. If you don't offer me more than that then we don't need to talk. You need to bring *you* to the product and product offering.

People and people skills are a major component of what it takes to be considered a great person in this industry. Being able to strike up a conversation at a moment's notice and turn someone's day around from a negative to a positive is vital. Essentially, you are a counsellor, a teacher, a parent, a guide and a fitness industry operator all rolled into one. Trust me, if you spend one or two months in any fitness based role you will see that. People will come to you with their problems, their issues and their concerns, no matter how big or small. You must listen to them. I struggled with the concept of people not giving 100% at work, yet later on I begrudgingly came to realise that some of those people *were* giving 100%. The difference lay in my expectations of what 100% looked like and from their point of view I was asking for something that was more like 500%. So now, I no longer employ people unless they can give 500%.

It is easier once you have the right people but getting a hold of them in the first place is the hard part. How easy is it when you get to pick your team? But you won't always have that luxury, sometimes you will be handed a team which you have to adapt and mould to your way of doing things. This can create a challenge, as while change is inevitable for newer people some of the others are stuck in a state of inertia from where they cannot adapt. Humans need to adapt to survive and thrive. If they don't adapt, then they will need to vacate their place.

The right person is not any particular type. You don't have to have a six pack, be tall, to come from a certain area and to have years of experience. All you need in order to be the right person, is to be coachable and willing. That is all. Be coachable, be willing. If you look at the team members you currently have on your books and they have neither of these traits, then you need to reassess why they are on your team. Ask yourself what you can do to either ensure they become coachable and willing or ask yourself how you can make them no longer part of your business.

Without the right people on the bus you will have tension and problems. You will have one person pressing the accelerator and one person the brake at the same time and both in contention with each other. If you think you have the wrong people on your bus, make sure they get off at the next stop. Better still; try to make sure that you don't let them on in the first place. Take a a long, hard look at the next candidate you are thinking of hiring and ask them something that shows that they might be coachable and willing. I have a litmus test I like to use for all new hires: I simply ask myself would they irritate me, if I got stuck in an elevator with them and I had to wait for 30 minutes (your phone is dead so you can't hide on Facebook). Could you hold a conversation with that person for 30 minutes? If they wouldn't irritate you and you believe they have the other two traits, well that is a great start! Apologies to anyone I have interviewed and not hired. I hope we never meet in an elevator!

Challenge

If you have a business with employees in your team, do a head count and ask yourself honestly are they coachable and are they willing? If you are your own business, if you are a sole trader or work for yourself, ask yourself are you coachable, are you willing?

If the answer to either question is no, then you need to think more about your hiring strategy and to plan for the future.

If it is you that is not adhering to these competencies, then you need to adapt. The wrong people will not get the right result.

We're not here to make friends

Too often I see people coming into management roles under the illusion that they can make and maintain friendships with staff members, along the way. They feel that even though they are managers they can still confide and put faith in the people who work for them or around them. They feel as though they should be able to speak freely to one another without any consequences, issues or problems. You can probably take a guess as to how this can play out: very badly for all involved. Always vent up!

I once had a *'leak'* within the chain and had to find out where it was coming from. At the time, I had an open door policy with the office staff, where all were included. In an effort to isolate the leak, sometimes I would tell some people something in confidence to see if and when I would hear it back. This piece of news was completely fabricated so if I heard it I would know where it had come from. Different staff would get different stories and I would wait to see which one would come back to me. It was an interesting way to find out where and when I would hear things back. Before I told a person something I would specifically state that the following was going to be 100% discrete and confidential conversation which could not leave these office walls, yet within hours I would hear it back with legs and tails added on. It just goes to show that you need one other strong characteristic in your people and that is honesty.

Trusting one another helps to build confidence. However, when people can't trust each other because of one person's breaking the chain of trust I had to act to neutralise this risk. My advice is act straight away if you see a situation like this cropping up within your business model. Because people play such a vital role in the development of your business and the happiness of your customers, the wrong people can ruin many a reputation. They can become toxic and detrimental to your success as well as a business risk generally. When threats are presented, you must neutralise them.

Thankfully, watching good managers grow into great leaders is something that I have been able to do in my time. What is the difference between a good manager and a great leader? It's a similar line to the one that comes between professionalism and friendship. Managers can be mates but leaders must be strong and avoid forming overtly strong relationships within the team, which can become hazardous. As hard as it might be, a leader will always do what *is right* not just what feels right at the time. They can see the bigger picture and thus can detach themselves from any overly emotional connotations in situations, where necessary.

Challenge

Complete a self-analysis and be critical of your recent actions: Have you possibly overstepped the line with a client: too many coffees, too casual maybe? If so re-evaluate and make sure that you are acting accordingly.

Succession planning

You ought to work so hard, that you would be irreplaceable if you left. That was always my logic during my career. I moved to Australia, initially, on a whim with a backpack and a few dollars but I only had one long term goal in mind: to become a resident. I began working with the company that eventually sponsored me. However when I was starting out I met numerous people on the same level as me who said that they couldn't get sponsored, even though they had been promised it and wanted it. Looking back, I don't think I would have sponsored those people either. At the time I thought to myself, *you* may not have got a sponsorship but *I am not you!* I had one plan and that was to work as diligently as possible, to work like a maniac, doing countless hours and achieving all the KPI's I was set. I would not rest until the job was done. A manic work rate which all came crashing down when I began to feel as though the sponsorship process was not moving as fast as it could. I did what any one would do, I took a gamble. The evening that I made up my mind, I sent an email to the two senior managers in the area for the company stating that I appreciated all their support and help, however due to lack of progression with the sponsorship I would have to resign and I officially gave my notice. I still work for this company by the way. It was risky because I didn't really have a back-up plan. I didn't know what would happen. But thankfully, it worked and within a few days the ball was rolling. Looking back now that was the best move that I ever made. It may well have happened anyway, but I forced the issue. Back yourself. If you feel as though you have what it takes to be that person in that role, tell the world and believe in yourself. Don't be dismayed by anyone else's take on the process, they know nothing about you!

I have carried this principle with me all throughout my career; working so hard that if you leave there will be a void. It's a manic work rate. Yet I have come to understand now, that in order to progress you must actually make yourself replaceable, as you climb the corporate ladder. If you are looking to step up to a senior management role, you must ensure one of your staff members is ready for your mid-management position and thus you can ensure a smooth handover. That fact will be running in the back of the recruiter's mind in any interview; who will I put into this person's seat? If you make that transition an easy one, it ensures your horizons are also broadened.

Succession planning begins when you have leaders who still want to grow, as all leaders should. You must begin to upskill and increase your team's power and prowess. Lead is part of the word *leader* and you must lead your people to become better people. The ones you hire should be the ones who want to sit in your seat, now.

Challenge

Create a succession plan based around the current team you have: it could be your own succession up the corporate ladder or the succession from work to retirement. How will you work your way up, to work your way out (if that's what you want!)

The Future

Change

The stories of Nokia, the Walkman and the VHS player - they should all scare you.

They should make you aware of the importance of change and staying ahead of it. If you don't stay current, you will become obsolete. To avoid falling victim to the destruction that can be 'change' you need to avoid inertia at all costs. You must accept change; you must adapt to it and get ahead of it. What can you do to remain current? Keep an eye on trends that are becoming widespread in your industry. If I look at the current state of affairs in the fitness industry at the moment, I can see some major shifts; one that is becoming a threat is that of a studio within a studio. Larger scale health clubs are encompassing smaller studios and are creating boutiques within the health club. It's a bit like stores within a shopping mall. This is one way in which the industry is changing, so how can you get ahead of this structural shift? Build it to sell it; build your business so that it can be swallowed up by a larger company. You can rent space from a larger facility at a lower cost and a lower risk.

The next shift which I am noticing is that of the 'wellness warrior'; people who live their entire lives based around fitness. They buy fitness equipment for at home, they train at a gym, they read fitness, they eat based on their health and fitness needs, they wear fitness brands and they are fully enveloped in the 'fitmosphere'. The fitmosphere is all-encompassing and is becoming a strong factor in people's buying decisions. How can you use this 'fitmosphere' to your advantage? What product offerings can you add to your marketing mix to ensure you have a hand in more than one segment of the fitmosphere?

The fitmosphere is made up of many segments based around five key areas:

1. Physical Fitness – Training the body to increase longevity and to ensure a winning physique.

2. Style and Branding – Fit brands, active wear products which help facilitate movement but keep style at the forefront of their mind. Rocky Balboa style grey sweat pants are no longer acceptable.

3. Mental and Learning outcomes – Staying current on trends, increasing their knowledge base about body musculature, exercise, nutrition and the rest. A strong mind and a strong body go hand in hand; this area is strong in mental health and a positive mind-set.

4. Food and Beverage – Organic products with 'clean' living at their core. If you use good fuel for your car, you use good food for your body.

5. Fun – fun activities revolving around getting active and where movement is a key component.

Change is good, if you face it head on and embrace it from the beginning. Keep your eye on these two main movers and shakers for the future: a boutique within a facility and the fitmosphere approach to your business.

The only thing you can be sure of is that there will be change. Change can either become the catalyst for success or a destructive force, based on the way in which we conduct our business on a day-to-day basis. Do you get ahead of the curve, stay current and try to look at what is coming around the corner? Do you try to ascertain what the next key momentum shift will look like? If you are doing that, you should give yourself a fighting chance. If you think about your business like you would any portfolio, the key to success is generally diversification; yet too often you pigeonhole yourself into just being one thing. You do not leave any room for manoeuvre; you are stuck as being this and nothing else. To be a *change business* you must be fluid and willing to flow in a new direction at a moment's notice.

In previous training seminars, I have used the metaphor of a river meandering along its path. As a river, it is in its mature stage; it sways from side to side often meandering far and wide across the plains over which it runs. The lifecycle of a business and a river have something in common, the path of least resistance is a term which can be related to both. If a river follows its path, in its mature stage, it will usually meander out wide until eventually that meander, that curve, becomes cut off from the rest of the body of water that flows straight through and then the flow of water to the curved section slows down. The alluvial soil is deposited at this point and it builds up and causes that section to become cut off - to become an ox-bow lake (or 'billabong' for the Aussies among us). The ox-bow lake eventually grows old and the water in it becomes stagnant. Thanks to my Geography teacher for drilling this into us all in school. This is what happens when you follow the path of least resistance in business, you dry up and die! Never take the easy route just because, you will never learn and you will never grow. Although it may be easier to follow that option, in the end you will be worse off. If it takes you a year longer, but you learn more and are more adaptable to change after that, then take that option no matter how fast the other option may be.

The Membership Mindset

Putting it all together

So where does that leave you after all is said and done? To operate at optimum efficiency, you need to operate from a position of a membership mindset and not a transactional thinking mindset. You want to ensure that you create continual revenues, not just one-off type payments. Moving away from transactional thinking and towards a membership mindset is the key to achieving this.

I hope that you have completed all of the challenges along the way and that you have gained some knowledge and know-how that you might not have been aware of prior to embarking on this journey with me. This was a journey for me too; a journey of too many Nespresso capsules, a lot of Chet Faker in the background and pages and pages of rewrites. We all learn as we go along and I am no different. If even one of you gets something from this book, then it has all been worth it.

Just to sum it up a little, I would say that in order for me to change the way I thought about my business offering and about what I do, I had to make sure I did the following things:

View customers as friends – make sure you treat them as such. No one sale is worth it, if it counts you out of further sales down the track. Make decisions today that will create a better tomorrow.

See the world as how you want it to be – remember the importance of self-talk. Instead of saying you are overwhelmed, say that you in a state of elevated learning. You see where I am going with this.

The right people will get the right results – you cannot succeed with people who are not 100% on board. If they do not believe in the product or in the approach they can go ahead and be non-believers but somewhere else, not in your business.

Embrace change – the only constant is, and always will be change. Do not shy away from it, prepare for it, be ready for it and adapt to it. Investigate your field and try to predict the future shifts in the industry. Look at what the 'share economy' has done to transport and hotels with Uber and Airbnb becoming strong players in both markets respectively.

Live in the fitmosphere – this is the new-age, all-encompassing fitness atmosphere where people's lives seem to revolve around the concept of health and fitness, from the lifestyle brands that they wear to the coffee shops which they drink at. Ensure you understand that a membership mindset means that you will have to consider all the strands of this fitmosphere. The fitmosphere can be summed up as an atmosphere where health and fitness permeate all layers of a person, dictating what they do, from the television they watch to the coffee they drink and at one stage or another; they will consider their health and fitness. Fun fitness fact: as I wrote this book I set myself a fitness challenge to do twenty push-ups after the completion of each chapter. A great way for me to incorporate fitness into what I do, safe to say my chest was pretty sore towards the end of the book's completion. Have fun and enjoy the process.

You are now fully versed on what it takes to be a fitness industry operator from the incubator stage right through to global success. Lots of other business models can implement the membership mindset, from massage to cinema, they can all take some wisdom from this way of operating and for this reason, you can now see some of these types of service providers delving into the membership economy. Ask yourself to complete all of the challenges honestly and see how much you can grow from Chapter One onwards. Everyone takes their own direction from this book; whichever way it takes you is the way that is meant. You are the captain of the ship; I am simply providing some beacons to guide you through to the harbour.

I wish you all the best in your fitness journey and remember to always test yourself, regardless of the position that you are in. Complacency within the industry is certain to cause catastrophes.

Now that you understand what we do, please visit www.membershipmindset.com.au to start learning live.

Find up to date information on seminars, coaching and exclusive programs/content.

Experience *The Membership Mindset* today!

INDEX